POLICY AND PRACTI(
NUMBER TWENTY-NINE
COACHING AND MENTORING:
DEVELOPING TEACHERS AND LEADERS

POLICY AND PRACTICE IN EDUCATION

1: Lindsay Paterson, *Education and the Scottish Parliament* (out of print)
2: Gordon Kirk, *Enhancing Quality in Teacher Education* (out of print)
3: Nigel Grant, *Multicultural Education in Scotland* (out of print)
4: Lyn Tett, *Community Education, Lifelong Learning and Social Inclusion* now published as *Community Education, Lifelong Learning and Development* (Third Edition 2010)
5: Sheila Riddell, *Special Educational Needs: Providing additional support* (Second edition, 2006)
6: J. Eric Wilkinson, *Early Childhood Education: The new agenda* (out of print)
7: Henry Maitles, *Values in Education: We're all citizens now* (out of print)
8: Willis Pickard and John Dobie, *The Political Context of Education after devolution* (out of print)
9: Jim O'Brien, Daniel Murphy and Janet Draper, *School Leadership* (Second Edition 2008)
10: Margaret Nicolson and Matthew MacIver (eds), *Gaelic Medium Education* (2003)
11: Gordon Kirk, Walter Beveridge and Iain Smith, *The Chartered Teacher* (out of print)
12: Jim O'Brien and Gale Macleod, *The Social Agenda of the School* (2009)
13: Ann Glaister and Bob Glaister (eds), *Inter-Agency Collaboration: Providing for children* (2005)
14: Mary Simpson, *Assessment* (out of print)
15: Ian Menter, Estelle Brisard and Ian Smith, *Convergence or Divergence? Initial teacher education in Scotland and England* (out of print)
16: Janet Draper and Jim O'Brien, *Induction: Fostering career development at all stages* (out of print)
17: Sheila Riddell and Lyn Tett, *Gender and Teaching: Where have all the men gone?* (2006)
18: George Head, *Better Learning, Better Behaviour* (2007)
19: Margaret Martin, *Building a Learning Community in the Primary Classroom* (2007)
20: Christine Forde (ed.), *Tackling Gender Inequality, Raising Pupil Achievement* (2007)
21: Daniel Murphy, *Professional School Leadership: Dealing with dilemmas* (2007)
22: Beth Dickson, *Education and the Arts* (2011)
23: Stephen J. McKinney (ed.), *Faith Schools in the Twenty-First Century* (2008)
24: Jenny Reeves and Alison Fox (eds), *Practice-Based Learning: Developing excellence in teaching* (2008)
25: Jeannie Mackenzie, *Family Learning: Engaging with parents* (2009)
26: Margery McMahon, *International Education: Educating for a global future* (2011)
27: Malcolm Thorburn and Shirley Gray, *Physical Education: Picking up the baton* (2009)
28: Annette Coburn and David Wallace, *Youth Work in Communities and Schools* (2011)
29: Christine Forde and Jim O'Brien (eds), *Coaching and Mentoring: Developing teachers and leaders* (2011)
30: Vivienne Baumfield, *Learning to Teach and Teaching to Learn* (2012)

POLICY AND PRACTICE IN EDUCATION
SERIES EDITORS
JIM O'BRIEN and **CHRISTINE FORDE**

COACHING AND MENTORING
Developing Teachers and Leaders

Edited by

Christine Forde

Professor of Leadership and Professional Learning,
School of Education,
University of Glasgow

and

Jim O'Brien

Professor Emeritus,
The Moray House School of Education,
University of Edinburgh

Published by
Dunedin Academic Press Ltd
Hudson House
8 Albany Street
Edinburgh EH1 3QB
Scotland

ISBN 978-1-906716-29-5
ISSN 1479-6910

British Library Cataloguing in Publication data
A catalogue record for this book is available from the British Library

Typeset by Makar Publishing Production, Edinburgh
Printed and bound in the United Kingdom
by CPI Antony Rowe, Chippenham and Eastbourne
Printed on paper from sustainable resources

CONTENTS

Series Editors' Introduction   v

Editors and Contributors   vi

Chapter 1: Teacher professional development: purpose,
policy and practice   1
Jim O'Brien

Chapter 2: Approaches to professional learning: coaching,
mentoring and building collaboration   17
Christine Forde

Chapter 3: Learning to teach: an examination of mentoring
in the Scottish teacher induction scheme   32
Margaret Martin

Chapter 4: Learning to lead: coaching, mentoring and tutoring in
leadership development   45
Deirdre Torrance

Chapter 5: Learning together: professional learning communities   63
Mike Carroll

Chapter 6: Taking continuing teacher education forward   82
Christine Forde and Jim O'Brien

References   91

Index   104

SERIES EDITORS' INTRODUCTION

Drawing from the international literature and more locally centred research and policy, this addition to the Policy and Practice in Education Series, coordinated and edited by the Series Editors, focuses on teacher professional learning and the contribution of coaching and mentoring. Substantial investment in the Continuing Professional Development (CPD) of teachers is evident over the past twenty years, but CPD, while commonplace in the lives of teachers, remains problematic in terms of policy, purpose and practice. Three key interactive and mutually independent processes of professional practice – namely, reflection, enquiry and critique – are posited as fundamental to bringing together the essential features of the professional learning process. These essential features are highlighted as professional practice, dialogue and support between professionals, and as ideas or knowledge derived from theory, policy, research or the experience of fellow professionals. The potential of Coaching and Mentoring to the professional learning process is recognised. Coaching and Mentoring have emerged as key elements in a number of the ways, both individual and collective, in which professional learning is addressed. Examples are provided with respect to preparing to teach, teacher induction and early professional development, professional learning communities, and the preparation and development of school leaders by Margaret Martin, Mike Carroll and Deirdre Torrance – contributors engaged in the day-to-day realities of such provision underpinned by their extensive research experience.

Dr Jim O'Brien
Professor Emeritus,
The Moray House School of Education,
The University of Edinburgh

Dr Christine Forde
Professor of Leadership and Professional
Learning, School of Education,
The University of Glasgow

EDITORS AND CONTRIBUTORS

Christine Forde is Professor of Leadership and Professional Learning in the School of Education at Glasgow University

Jim O'Brien is Professor Emeritus of Leadership and Professional Learning in the Moray House School of Education at Edinburgh University

Margaret Martin is a Senior Lecturer in the School of Education at Glasgow University

Deirdre Torrance is a Lecturer in Educational Leadership in the Moray House School of Education at Edinburgh University

Mike Carroll is a Lecturer in the School of Education at Glasgow University

CHAPTER 1

Teacher professional development: purpose, policy and practice

Jim O'Brien

Introduction

National educational systems invariably have differing priorities and emphases, but teacher professional development or learning is universally considered to be a key component in any planned systemic change related to a new curriculum or organisational or governance initiative. In the United Kingdom, in the past 25 years, governments of varying political hue, as a priority, have sought through policy intervention to change teachers' professionalism with a view to raise standards and student achievement. There have been few occasions when major innovations have not been associated with a Continuing Professional Development (CPD) programme for teachers.

In 1997, with the election of a 'New Labour' government at Westminster, the national governance of education changed substantially. The Westminster Parliament retained responsibility for education policy in England. However, the subsequent devolution settlement, with the establishment of the Scottish Parliament (Paterson, 2000) and Assemblies in Northern Ireland (Montgomery and Smith, 2006) and Wales (Daugherty, 2006; Rees, 2007), means that is where policy responsibility now rests.

This chapter focuses on the purposes, policy development and resultant practice associated with teacher CPD and attempts to trace the developments and underlying theories that have led to a current belief in the efficacy of a 'coaching and mentoring' approach to teacher personal and professional growth. While United Kingdom developments will be informed by consideration of the international literature, the author writes from the perspective of someone who has always worked and researched in the Scottish context and examples used will inevitably originate from there, especially given the resurgence of interest in the 'distinctiveness' of Scottish education (Bryce and Humes, 2008; Raffe, 2004; Ozga, 2005; Arnott and Ozga, 2010) and with comparisons (Raffe *et al.*, 1999; Phillips, 2003) of the developing arrangements in a devolved United Kingdom.

Substantial government investment in the professional development of teachers and, more recently, the expanding school workforce can be identified. Provision for associated professional learning in the induction programme enjoyed by Newly Qualified Teachers (NQTs) in Scottish schools (O'Brien and Christie, 2005; O'Brien, 2009) or the extensive work done by the National College for Leadership of Schools and Children's Services (NCLSCS – formerly National College for School Leadership [NCSL]) in England and Wales are only two examples.

In-service training (INSET) and Continuing Professional Development (CPD)

Continuing professional development (CPD) appears a relatively straightforward concept underpinned by the provision of training or experiences with the aim of ultimately improving student learning. However, in the literature there are issues with terminology. Some people refer to CPD as 'Continuing', others as 'Continuous', while 'teacher development' or 'professional growth' are other terms in use, whereas my own preferred, but now only emerging phrase, especially in the Australian published research, is 'professional learning'. Without explicit definition, such phrases are as a result interchangeable in much of the literature, but they can mean different things (Bolam and McMahon, 2004). We have moved on from initial notions of in-service training (INSET), which often involved planned activities, especially courses, both in and out of school designed to prepare for specific innovations or to enhance professional knowledge, skills, attitudes and teacher performance. Much sound advice (often more ignored than observed) was provided by the James Report (DES, 1972; Taylor, 2008):

> In-service training should begin in the schools. It is here that learning and teaching take place, curriculum and techniques are developed and needs and deficiencies revealed. Every school

should regard the continued training of its teachers as an essential part of its task, for which all members of staff share responsibility. An active school is constantly reviewing and reassuring its effectiveness and is ready to consider new methods, new forms of organizational and new ways of dealing with the problems that arise.

For many teachers INSET involved compulsory training days ('Baker Days' in England, named after an Education Secretary in the Thatcher government) managed by local education authority advisers or senior school management.

As noted, a plethora of interchangeable terms exist, but there have been attempts to define some terms. For example, when 'staff development' was the in-vogue term, Hewton (1988) indicated that the principal purpose of staff development is to enhance the quality of pupils' learning, and suggested:

> A staff development programme is a planned process of development which enhances the quality of pupil learning by identifying, clarifying and meeting the individual needs of the staff within the context of the institution as a whole. (p. 89)

While Kerwood and Clements (1986, p. 211) opined:

> Staff development embraces not only individual education and training, individual appraisal and career enhancement, but also whole-staff development as part of a dynamic and changing organisation. Unlike curriculum development which can be subject specific and limited in scope, staff development is more than improving teaching technique within a subject area: it includes all-round development of the individual and the inter-relationships of teachers' different subject areas and levels of responsibility.

Fullan (1991, p. 123) stressed the importance of teacher development: 'Continuous development of all teachers is the cornerstone for meaning, improvement and reform. Professional development and school development are inextricably linked.'

However, Evans (2002) argues that the concept of teacher development remains ill-defined and unclear. Her examination of the concept (pp. 124–9) reveals that many authors 'fail to offer definitions of teacher development or of professional development'. This leads to queries about whether professional development is a process or a product. Evans suggests that much writing on teacher development focuses more on '… describing the situations and circumstances that they consider to have been the vehicles for specific cases of teacher development': for example, workshops, study groups, professional reading and discussions with other teachers. Policy in this field may as a result suffer through such lack of conceptual clarity. It is true also of other professions as Friedman and Phillips (2004, pp. 362–3) confirm: 'There is confusion regarding its [CPD] definition and purpose in both academic and practitioner literature, which extends to professionals themselves.' Such vagueness results in a situation where

> CPD promises to deliver strategies of learning that will be of benefit to individuals, foster personal development, and produce professionals who are flexible, self-reflective and empowered to take control of their own learning. This emphasis on the personal, however, could conflict with concepts of CPD as a means of training professionals to fulfill specific work roles and as a guarantee of individual, professional competence.

Friedman and Phillips indicate that 40% of UK professional associations had adopted the definition formulated by the Construction Industry Council (1986, p. 3), namely:

> CPD is the systematic maintenance, improvement and broadening of knowledge and skill and the development of personal qualities necessary for the execution of professional and technical duties throughout the practitioner's working life.

For teachers, Day (1999, p. 4) conceptualises CPD in a way that is accepted by many commentators:

> Professional development consists of all natural learning experiences and those conscious and planned activities which are intended to be of direct or indirect benefit to the individual, group or school and which contribute through these to the quality of education in the classroom. It is the process by which, alone and with others, teachers review, renew and extend their

commitment as change agents to the moral purposes of teaching; and by which they acquire and develop critically the knowledge, skills and emotional intelligence essential to good professional thinking, planning and practice with children, young people and colleagues through each phase of their teaching lives.

In the policy milieu, the GTCW (2002, p.17) adopted a wide but brief definition: 'Professional Development encompasses all formal and informal learning which enables teachers to improve their own practice.'

Education reform

Schooling and, as a result, teacher education in the United Kingdom, have been subject to considerable reform since the Callaghan Ruskin College speech (Callaghan, 1976) signalled serious concerns about educational standards. Post 1979, the ideas espoused by Keith Joseph and the 'New Right' and put into practice during the 'Thatcher era', especially in England and Wales, were critical, although Scotland was far from immune (Arnott, 2011). For example, developments such as enhanced governing bodies (the Scottish equivalent was the introduction of School Boards), the local management of schools (devolved school management in Scotland), a national curriculum, schools 'opting out' of LEA control, the introduction of regular and rigorous external inspections, teacher appraisal and the strengthening of standards or competences for teachers (Mahony and Hextall, 2000) were established. There was no let up as such developments and innovations continued unabated under New Labour (Furlong *et al.*. 2000), because the prevailing orthodoxy demanded that public services become efficient and effective by adopting the practices and approaches used by business. In England, increased government intervention and control through prescription and accountability became the 'norm'. Tony Blair viewed the teaching profession as critical to achieving increased student standards and more effective schools, and stated in the 1998 Green Paper outlining the future:

> education is this government's top priority. The teaching profession is critical to our mission ... this Green Paper sets out the government's proposals to improve the teaching profession ... [It represents] the most fundamental reform of the teaching profession since state education began. (Tony Blair in DfEE, 1998, p. 5)

Such modernisation, or 'New Professionalism' as it became known, is discussed by Day (2002, 2005), who provides interesting insights into the influences specifically on school leadership policy as he 'charts the changes over the last 20 years of government policies and the effects of the new performativity agendas' (2005, p. 393). Much of his identification of pressures on the system holds true in the rest of the UK, although similar changes may not have been so overt or have plainly not been adopted, for example in Scotland, where collaboration between schools has continued to be a priority and the creation of a quasi-market associated with schools opting out and raising standards has failed to take hold. Interestingly, a market in professional development emerged and with it a proliferation of providers. Day and Gu (2007, pp. 424–5) claim:

> In summary, performativity agendas, coupled with the continuing monitoring of the efficiency with which teachers are expected to implement externally generated initiatives, have had five consequences. They have:
> (i)   implicitly encouraged teachers to comply uncritically (for example, teach to the test so that teaching becomes more a technical activity and thus more susceptible to control);
> (ii)   challenged teachers' substantive identities;
> (iii) reduced the time teachers have to connect with, care for and attend to the needs of individual students;
> (iv)   threatened teachers' sense of agency and resilience;
> (v)   challenged teachers' capacities to maintain motivation, efficacy and thus, commitment.

Does this suggest that professional development policy and available provision also played a part in such alienation?

Major CPD policy initiatives since 1997

One cannot discuss policy initiatives in teacher professional development without considering issues of purpose or assumptions. Conlon (2004, pp. 116–20), in an article critiquing the New Opportunities Fund (a major UK-wide New Labour policy) and its approach to teacher professional development in ICT, summarises the important contributions of Day (1999), Dadds (1997) and Harland and Kinder (1997) to our understanding of CPD.

For teachers, the effectiveness of CPD hangs on the conditions under which opportunities for development actually result in changes in classroom practice. Harland and Kinder (1997) suggest that up to nine outcomes must be present, either pre-existing or following an in-service event: material and provisionary outcomes, informational outcomes, new awareness, value congruence, affective and motivational outcomes, attitudinal outcomes, knowledge and skills, institutional outcomes and impact on practice. In the three-tier hierarchy of outcomes they propose that *value congruence*, when a teacher's personal values about what constitutes good teaching match the message about best practice being promulgated in the professional development, and *knowledge and skills* are 'first order' outcomes (p. 77). Their research indicated that teachers follow an individual path through the outcomes, the implication being that the same in-service event will lead to different outcomes for different participants. With respect to Harland and Kinders' seminal outcomes-based analysis of CPD and their formulation of nine outcomes outlined, Conlon (2004, p. 118) illustrates the hierarchical nature of these outcomes thus:

Impact on Practice

Value Congruence   **Knowledge and Skills**

Motivation   **Affective**   **Institutional**

Provisionary   **Information**   **Awareness**

Conlon acknowledges that other writers just as importantly focus more on process-based outcomes. He indicates that Dadds argues that

> major educational reform initiatives in England have been based on 'empty vessel' or 'delivery' models in which the teacher is positioned as the uncritical implementer of outside policies? These models have been harmful for several reasons:
>
> - They assume erroneously that 'good practice' will come about from those outside schools making judgments for and on those inside.
> - They have little to say about the crucial role of teachers' understandings about children.
> - They have nothing to say about the variety and complexity of processes that teachers undergo as they continue to learn about their professional craft.
> - They do not fully account for the complexities of the curriculum as experienced by children, as teachers mediate

between reforms and the needs of unique learners. (Conlon, 2004, p. 119)

Conlon suggests Day argues that teachers need to be centrally involved in the conduct of CPD as active agents in determining what and how they may learn. This will be emotionally satisfying and will secure teacher commitment. Day's recommendations include the use of collaborative approaches, including action research and critical friendships, the promotion of school cultures in which head teachers are not just managers, but also leaders who promote shared ownership of a professional learning culture, and collaborative networks internal and external to the school.

In the 1980s and 1990s, for most teachers the experience of 'formal' professional development, was related to planned education authority or in-school activity. In Scotland, this provision was aligned with the aims and targets of individual school development plans. CPD provision was available nationally for the appraisal initiative (staff development and review) and extensive management training was provided for head teachers. The vast majority of Scottish teachers did not take additional qualifications despite the emergence of systems of accrediting experience involving new and professionally oriented but elective and voluntary Masters and Postgraduate Diploma/Certificate awards in the then Colleges of Education which all subsequently merged with universities. There was a growing policy suggestion that such an unplanned model of professional development was inadequate (Sutherland, 1997).

Raising student standards and curricular change were key areas for professional development. Furlong (2005, p. 129) indicates that in England,

> What the 1998 Green Paper argued for was the need to balance different sorts of training needs. There should be a balance between responding to:
> - *National* training priorities focused on particular needs, which have been identified nationally, e.g. literacy, numeracy, ICT, headship training, special educational needs;
> - *School* priorities emerging from school development planning to help schools reach their own targets and implement their post Ofsted action plans; and
> - *Individual* development needs of teachers identified through annual appraisal. (para. 123)

The possibility of study leave and extended sabbaticals for teacher development were mooted in response to this declaration of the importance of addressing individual needs, but little subsequently materialised with the limited exception of the Best Practice Research Scholarship scheme, abandoned for economic reasons in 2003–4. Subsequently there have been a number of policy announcements and reviews of CPD in England (DfEE, 2001; CUREE for DfES, 2005; Ofsted, 2004, 2006; TDA, 2009) and separately in Wales (National Assembly for Wales, 2001; GTCW, 2006).

In England, the introduction of the national strategies for literacy and numeracy were accompanied by an ambitious national programme of training which saw a 'cascade' model of training being developed. Overall, CPD rapidly focused on supporting performance management, with schools becoming the focal point of CPD both in terms of identifying needs and providing for such needs from within. An increasing emphasis on mentoring and coaching is discernible in this process as a part of the normal lives of teachers. Additionally, a national framework of professional standards for teachers emerged (TDA, 2006) clearly underpinned by the discourse of *performativity*.

This approach is not supported by all. Brighouse (2008, p. 321) argues that teachers flourish best when four needs are met. Teachers

- are given *responsibility*; that is, are recognised as the trusted expert and offering leadership of teaching, assessment, curriculum or school organisation;
- enjoy *permitting circumstances*; through leadership of the department, the phase or the school in which they teach they must be permitted to take risks without subsequent blame and encouraged by professional dialogue;
- are afforded *respect and recognition*; where there is deserved appreciation of their efforts in the school, the local community and further afield.
- are offered *new experiences*; regular opportunities to see others doing similar and different jobs, access to subject association meetings, courses, conferences, and opportunities to study and to research, reflect and enhance professional practice.

In England the national framework for mentoring and coaching (CUREE, 2005) was designed to support those wanting to develop mentoring and coaching within their school. The framework covered:

- principles of mentoring and coaching;
- core concepts for mentoring, specialist coaching and collaborative (co-) coaching;
- skills needed for mentoring and coaching;
- a comparison between mentoring and different forms of coaching.

It is evident that coaching increasingly becomes viewed as a necessary part of CPD provision and it is again emphasised in the Teachers Development Agency (2009) strategy for developing the children's workforce in schools. This strategy sets out three priorities:

Priority one: embed a learning culture

PD leaders, at all levels, promote a learning culture in which the whole school workforce has a right to sustained and effective PD, focused on improvement, that has a positive impact on the achievements and life chances of all children and young people.

Schools lead and sustain their own improvement, make a clear link between individual and team PD and school improvement, and use induction and performance review processes to plan and provide PD for the whole school workforce.

Priority two: increase coherence and collaboration

Opportunities for collaboration at local, regional and national levels are increased, reducing duplication and bringing greater coherence, challenge and sustainability to PD practice.

Schools and other children's services share good practice and work and learn together to meet PD needs in ways that will improve outcomes for children and young people.

Priority three: improve quality and capacity

Capacity building in and across schools makes best use of available resources, including technology and finance. Schools lead and sustain improvement. All PD is high quality, informed by research and best practice, judged and evaluated on its impact on children and young people and value for money, and meets school-specific and individual needs.

Members of the school workforce develop the skills needed for the twenty-first century schools system. They can access PD opportunities and qualifications that support the development of individual practice and career progression within the school and across the children's work-force. (p. 13)

These are ambitious priorities, but with the 2010 election of the Coalition Government elements such as the Masters in Teaching and Learning (MTL) have already been abandoned. However, it appears that collaboration, coaching and the notion of learning communities are now the mainstays of professional learning in schools in England.

Policies in Wales have piloted and espoused Professional Development Bursaries, Visit and Exchanges and Teacher Research Scholarships – a similar scheme exists in Scotland (GTCS 2011a). By 2004 in Wales, over 6,000 teachers had used bursaries to undertake activities such as attending courses, visiting schools, pursuing higher degrees or involvement in projects in their own schools. Some 450 teachers had visited schools across the world to view and share good practice, while 400 teachers had undertaken action research projects by accessing scholarships. Over 8,000 teachers in 450 schools were funded under a whole-staff CPD initiative in the same period. The General Teaching Council for Wales (GTCW) had been invited to develop a CPD framework, and their (2006, p. 7) advice document reported positive progress on the initial four main strands of interrelated work:

- career progression – professional milestones and standards;
- professional development, recognition and accreditation;
- recording of professional development and self-reflection;
- quality assurance of providers.

The advice suggested that there remained a 'Lack of clarity and consistency in the professional development opportunities open to teachers or most appropriate as they progress through their careers' (p. 13). The challenge remained to identify 'any gaps in the existing national professional development arrangements, so as to ensure that all teachers receive high-quality professional development, from the start to the end of their careers, regardless of factors such as the sector in which they work, geographic location, length of service or limitations in funding.' (p. 14). Council's advice sought to bring together issues of national standards (these existed for Qualified Teacher Status, Induction and Headship) for teacher CPD and professional recognition (distinct from any HE award available), and to introduce the Welsh version of a standard for Chartered Teacher which had emerged some years earlier in Scotland, where the past decade has witnessed the emergence of a CPD framework (Christie, 2003; Christie and O'Brien, 2005; O'Brien, 2007; Purdon, 2003, 2004; Kennedy, 2007) in a piecemeal fashion.

Without an equivalent of the Teachers Development Agency, Scotland relied on achieving a professional consensus with respect to a learning framework based on standards. Standards detail the competences expected at different stages of a teacher's career and provide a framework for associated programmes of CPD. Often associated with rhetoric about greater teacher professionalism, standards have generated misgivings internationally, especially about the effect on professional autonomy. For example, Tickle (2001), writing of the original English Induction Standards, expressed concerns that they reflected too narrow a view of teacher expertise. Patrick *et al.* (2003) identify competing discourses in Scottish education, *performativity* versus *autonomy* and *managerialism* versus *pedagogic excellence.* By conceptualising teaching in simplistic terms as a set of measurable outcomes, they suggest the CPD framework may undermine the autonomy and professionalism that it claims to increase. Why Scottish policymakers chose the path of professional development through standards has never been articulated. Purdon does express suspicions that such a framework permits closer political control over teachers' lives. As with other jurisdictions within the UK beyond the QTS standard, Scotland now has standards for Teacher Induction (Draper *et al.*, 2005), Chartered Teachers (O'Brien and Hunt, 2005) and School Headship (Cowie, 2005).

The need for an appropriate context for development has not been made explicit in the Scottish CPD Framework which appears to 'focus on teacher development as an individual enterprise' (Reeves *et al.*, 2002, p. 33). Perhaps that is why there is a developing interest in collaboration (Kennedy, 2011), communities of practice and teacher inquiry especially in relation to the new Scottish curriculum – A Curriculum for Excellence (Hulme *et al.*, 2009; Priestley *et al.*, 2011; Reeves, 2008).

How successful has CPD policy been in practice?

Alongside policy dissatisfaction with much professional development a decade ago has grown both an appreciation of the need for teachers to be committed to lifelong learning and a developing understanding of the nature of more effective CPD. The importance placed on CPD in the post-McCrone (SEED, 2001) changes to teachers' professional conditions of service in Scotland stemmed from a Scottish Executive Education

Department (SEED), analysis (2000, p. 8) of the challenges teachers had to face in an increasingly fast-paced world:

> The rapid changes that have taken place in many subjects; changes in the curriculum and teaching methods; development in technology, particularly information and communications technology; and the constantly evolving role of schools in our society, all mean that a teacher's competences and knowledge need frequently to be reviewed and updated.

Teaching work practices have changed and will continue to change, and curriculum development remains a constant in teachers' lives. Earlier curricular developments in Scotland such as the *5–14 Programme* and *Higher Still* provided opportunities for teachers to update their own knowledge, skills and expertise. The Scottish Office Education and Industry Department (SOEID) (1998) view was that teachers have a duty to maintain their professional learning and keep up to date with developments. Career advancement can be an inducement to engage wholeheartedly with CPD and, of course, as teachers gain experience, many will seek opportunities or new roles within schools that often require them of necessity to develop their knowledge and skills in order to take on and to be successful in new roles.

Evidence from a range of professions indicates that effective CPD requires an appropriate support infrastructure and that expectations should be clearly laid out by professional organisations (Friedman *et al.*, 1999; Phillips *et al.*, 2002). However, as we have noted, CPD activities will rarely be developmental unless they take on 'real personal value' for participants; engage with the purposes of the teacher and are sustained and followed up. Feiman-Nemser (2001) stresses that real teacher development needs to be based on serious teacher talk grounded in a professional community, and is often informal and day-to-day.

There have been a number of reviews of CPD in England, and several, including that of Hustler *et al.* (2003) were considered by Bolam and Weindling (2006). Adopting Day's (1999) definition of CPD quoted above, they presented findings from a systematic review of 20 research studies of teacher CPD in England published between 2002 and 2006. The conclusions of their review and analysis identified several issues:

- teacher development, learning and agency;
- new professionalism;

- schools' capacity for promoting effective professional development;
- external support for CPD and networking.

Their final issue was national CPD policy itself. They 'were impressed by the 2001 strategy document which set out CPD policy with coherence and clarity, while simultaneously demonstrating its integral links with broader education policy' (p. 122). However, they concluded that the DfES (2001) strategy

> is, historically, the exception; normally policy on CPD features as a part of strategy documents dealing with other, wider aspects of education policy and/or as a backdrop to operational and planning papers about CPD. This is more or less the current situation. (p. 122)

Kennedy's potentially seminal article (2005) indicates that we still have a long way to go in terms of providing appropriate CPD. She

> examines a range of models of CPD and proposes a framework through which they can be analysed. This analysis focuses on the perceived purpose of each model, identifying issues of power in relation to central control, individual teacher autonomy and profession-wide autonomy. (p. 236)

She discusses the purpose of CPD:

> that it can serve either to equip teachers with the requisite skills to implement such reforms as decided by others (usually government) or to inform, contribute to and provide critique of the reforms themselves. (pp. 247–8)

Nine models of CPD are identified and illustrated with examples and commentary on their efficacy and drawbacks: training; award-bearing; deficit; cascade; standards-based; coaching/ mentoring; community of practice; action research; transformative. She identifies such models as having characteristics associated with three purposes: namely, transmission, transitional and transformative. A warning is sounded that 'even within many collaborative forms of CPD ... the parameters of the activity are defined by some external party, usually in a position of power' (p. 148).

Despite a range of CPD models being recognised, the most recent survey report of the state of CPD in England (Opfer *et al.*, 2008) and

subsequent research journal articles (Opfer and Pedder, 2010, 2011) identify a series of issues which continue to suggest that a narrow range of
CPD opportunities are available to teachers and these vary significantly by
experience, career stage and leadership responsibility; barriers to teacher
participation still exist, including conditions in individual schools and the
perceptions held of CPD by teachers; most teachers' approaches to CPD
tend not to be collaborative, research-informed or located in classroom
practice despite the literature recommendations on such; passive learning
still appears to be the norm and CPD activities remain episodic and are
rarely rigorously evaluated; little impact on student standards is evident
and CPD remains centred on personal development. One might be pes-
simistic, therefore, when considering the successes and change effected by
CPD policy in the UK. Of course there are pockets of excellence, particularly in individual schools, and the UK is not alone in not achieving its
overall objectives with respect to teacher CPD. Darling-Hammond *et al.*
(2009) report on the state of CPD in the USA. Like much of the UK literature, the Report confirms what is known from research. For example:
'Effective professional development is intensive, ongoing, and connected
to practice; focuses on the teaching and learning of specific academic content; is connected to other school initiatives; and builds strong working
relationships among teachers' (p. 5), but again this is not uniformly available. Unfortunately, 'the United States is far behind in providing public
school teachers with opportunities to participate in extended learning opportunities and productive collaborative communities' (p. 6).

Why coaching and mentoring?
It would appear that coaching and mentoring may be critical as a key
means of promoting professional learning and social interaction utilising
the context and often the location of the school. In the rest of this book
Christine Forde's chapter considers the use of experiential approaches
to professional learning and growth and examines coaching and mentoring, peer-supported learning and the concept of professional learning communities. She places these alongside other pedagogies evident in
professional learning, that of tutoring and facilitation. The experience of
mentoring when entering the teaching profession may well shape teacher
perceptions of CPD for the remainder of their career and Margaret Martin's chapter follows with an examination of the nature and practice of
mentoring in the Scottish teacher induction scheme, a scheme which

has received the accolade of being described as 'world- class'. Leadership development is the key theme of the chapter by Deirdre Torrance as she guides us through the developing role of mentoring, tutoring and coaching in Scottish head teacher preparation. Subsequently, Mike Carroll returns to the question of professional learning communities, teasing out differences of meaning around the concept; the challenges and opportunities they offer for teacher CPD. In the final chapter the editors reflect on issues raised throughout the book and consider how continuing teacher education and professional learning can be taken forward.

CHAPTER 2

Approaches to professional learning: coaching, mentoring and building collaboration

Christine Forde

Introduction

This chapter examines the use of experiential methodologies in continuing teacher education in Scotland. While short-course-based provision continues, experiential forms of professional development have been adopted as part of programmes leading to professional qualifications (particularly the Chartered Teacher Programme and the Scottish Qualification for Headship), and in many local authority and school-based developments. Some of these approaches, notably coaching and mentoring, emphasise the importance of the individual development of teachers, while other approaches emphasise the importance of collaboration including peer-supported learning and professional learning communities (PLC) where the focus is on teachers developing and sharing their expertise. There is a danger that with the proliferation of schemes and variations in practice, we lose sight of some of the critical features and underpinning principles of these various approaches to professional learning. DuFour (2004), for example, concerned about very different activities being classed as 'professional learning communities', argues that we need to maintain a clarity of both definition and the underpinning purpose of this approach, an argument that could be applied to each of the approaches discussed here.

This chapter focuses initially on four approaches to professional development: mentoring, coaching, peer-supported learning and professional learning communities. Although these terms are evident in policy on professional development, they are often used interchangeably and loosely.

However, these are ideas and sets of practices whose legitimacy as effective processes for professional learning need to be examined critically. Much of the literature on these forms of professional learning provides guidance about how to coach or mentor or how to establish a professional learning community, but there is only limited discussion of how we define these practices and, more importantly, the underpinning assumptions about the nature of professional learning and practice that underpin these various practices. In this chapter we begin the critical appraisal of these ideas and practices. Further implicit in the increasing use of experiential pedagogies is a suggestion that what is important in the development of professional practice is largely 'experience'. However, the place of the development of philosophy and knowledge as part of the process of professional learning needs also to be considered. In the final part of this chapter we will consider the place of the development of wider sets of understandings relating to values and principles which shape practice, and pedagogies which support this development.

Professional learning

Experienced practitioners frequently provide a 'listening ear' and emotional support to their less-experienced colleagues. Further, teachers collaborate in areas such as curriculum development, teaching and school events. Although such practices have long existed, they have often been undertaken informally or have been viewed simply as tasks to produce, for example, a programme of study or a policy, rather than opportunities for teacher learning. However, research and recent policy have led to such activities now being understood as powerful approaches to promote teacher development (Forde *et al.*, 2006). In efforts to foster effective teacher learning there has been an expansion of the use of experiential methodologies in Scottish continuing teacher education, including mentoring, coaching, peer-supported learning and professional learning communities.

The use of experiential methodologies in pre-service and continuing education is evident across a variety of professional settings including medicine, business, nursing and engineering, as well as across different sectors and roles in education. Though there are some similarities in the processes of learning in different contexts, the application of these methods rests on an often unquestioned assumption about what it is to be a professional in a particular field or context. We can see this in an interesting contrast in the purpose of coaching and mentoring between education and business; whereas in education these processes are seen as opportunities for reflection on practice, in business there is much more emphasis on these processes for career development and advancement (Daresh, 2004). This idea of 'the reflective practitioner' is a cornerstone of teacher education and the practice of teaching (Calderhead and Gates, 1993) and at the core of these various learning processes such as coaching, mentoring, critical friendships or learning communities is the opportunity, the time, space and context to support critical reflection. Crucial here is the collaboration with others, because the creation of a genuine learning community can have a profound impact on pupil achievement.

While these are powerful methodologies for professional growth, we need also to consider the idea of reflective practice and its central role in teacher learning. This issue takes us right back to a consideration of the nature of teaching. In Scotland the founding document for the programme of curriculum reform known as the Curriculum for Excellence contained a clear statement about the central importance of teachers being 'the people best placed to make judgments about the learning needs of individual young people are those who work closely with them' (SE 2004, p. 14). However, the underlining of teachers' and schools' 'professional freedom' (SE 2004, p. 14) in these matters raises the question of what we mean by teaching. Timperley *et al.* (2007) point clearly to the fact that pupil learning is strongly influenced by what and how a teacher teaches, but we cannot reduce teaching to a simple set of skills and routines in the classroom. Instead, as Timperley *et al.* argue, we need to see teaching as a complex and theoretically informed activity, and that a strong theoretical basis is the foundation for principled decisions about the learning needs of individual pupils and groups of pupils and the ways of addressing these. Further, teachers need skills to inquire into the impact of their teaching on learning. Thus the idea of reflective practice then has to be imbued with ideas of self-evaluation, enquiry into practice and critical exploration of practice and experience set against theoretically sound principles, in order to make judgements about teaching and learning. This wider construction of teaching then raises questions about the place of theory and knowledge building side by side with experiential pedagogies. In the next sections we will explore some of examples of experiential pedagogies in professional learning, before discussing the relationship between these pedagogies and other pedagogies to be found in professional learning such as tutoring and facilitation.

Mentoring

Mentoring as a structured approach to professional learning can be a powerful process. Formal mentoring in education typically has a set duration, is used at key transition points in a teacher's career, and can include a range of activities such as learner-driven meetings, shadowing of the mentor by the learner, observation of practice and the use of reflective tools such as journals. Important in mentoring programmes is the dynamic relationship between mentor and learner as the learner moves from novice to peer, with the outcome of a mentoring process being the development of an autonomous professional.

Ganser (2006) highlights the widespread use of mentoring programmes for new teachers, which have a thirty-year history, and these programmes have been particularly associated with attempts to retain newly qualified teachers (Daresh (2004). Formal mentoring in the USA is also associated with preparation for and induction into headship, partly to address concerns for recruitment and retention of school principals as well as the drive for school effectiveness, and we can see similar approaches in the UK. In Scottish education mentoring has been used notably as a means to support two particular groups: firstly, aspiring and newly appointed headteachers, including in the Scottish Qualification for Headship (SQH) and secondly, newly qualified teachers during their induction year.

There are considerable strengths in mentoring, with the expertise of an experienced practitioner being drawn on to develop a novice, and benefits have been seen to accrue to both learner and mentor and, in some instances, the wider organisation. In their survey, Ehrich *et al.* (2004) identified that the most frequently cited benefits for learners were emotional aspects such as 'support, empathy, encouragement, counseling and friendship' (p. 523), but other benefits were also regularly noted such as support for classroom teaching, opportunities for discussion with a colleague and getting feedback and constructive criticism on practice. Ganser (2006) points to the need to further conceive of mentoring not just as a means of enabling a novice to cope with a new situation or role through psychological support or help with technical issues but to recognise the important affiliative dimensions of this process: 'the human, person-to-person dimension of mentoring and the very powerful connection between teachers that mentoring can engender' (p. 48). Findings from Ehrich *et al.*'s (2004) analysis of over three hundred studies of mentoring indicate that, while there are many attractive elements, we cannot, however, lose sight of how complex the role of mentor is and some of the tensions in particular schemes. A more informal approach to mentoring can lead to circumstances where there is a reliance on the goodwill of the participants rather than specific resourcing available to support this. Where there is insufficient resourcing, mentoring becomes a source of frustration and pressure for the mentor and feelings of being neglected on the part of the learner, which clearly can have a wider impact. The matching of mentor and learner is a second source of concern, and here matching may be in terms of personal compatibility but a more important consideration is the expertise of the mentor. The mentor draws from their own professional experience and skill to guide and support the learner and so there is a clear advisory, instructional element of mentoring. The mentor therefore needs to have credibility and expertise in these areas.

Coaching

The question of expertise is a critical feature of mentoring which stands in sharp contrast to some models of coaching. In some programmes coaches do not necessarily have to have expertise in the area of practice, and indeed in some models of 'executive coaching' (a form of coaching used predominantly in business with aspirant and experienced managers), being outside a particular domain is seen as an advantage enabling the coach to take an objective stance. The main distinction frequently drawn between mentoring and coaching is the directive nature of mentoring and the non-directive approach of coaching (Ives, 2008). Wales's (2002) examination of a coaching process used in business organisations argues that the goals of coaching should be internal, with the development of the learner's self-awareness and confidence being central, which leads to change in the learner's practice. In coaching, the development process rests on the coach providing feedback on what they observe or hear to enable the learner critically to reflect on their own practice. Importantly, this is not evaluatory feedback – judgement is suspended – but instead this feedback is likened to providing a mirror. The coach's task then is to enable the 'learner' to draw on his or her own resources to address issues in order to improve performance.

In education, coaching is frequently combined with other activities such as taught sessions, group discussions, networking and school-based activities in a range of leadership development programmes: for aspiring headteachers (Gronn *et al.*, 2008, Earley *et al.* 2008, Forde *et al.* forthcoming), newly appointed headteachers (Hanbury, 2009) and for middle leaders (Simkins *et al.* 2006), while Blackman (2010) looks at coaching and teacher leadership. Similar benefits were found across these programmes. Hanbury (2009), for example, found a number of strengths including personalisation of support and increased confidence where the learners were encouraged to express views and to find their own solutions to challenges in leadership.

While coaching is most often associated with leadership development, there are examples of coaching being used to support the development of teachers in their classroom practice. Coaching has been established in Scottish schools as a process to improve classroom practice (National CPD Team, n.d.). In Holland Veenman *et al.* (2001) developed coaching with supervising teachers who worked with the newly qualified teachers. Finding a number of limitations of mentoring in induction programmes, particularly an overemphasis on craft knowledge and the limited impact there seemed to be overall on newly qualified teachers' thinking and performance, the coaching of the student teachers offered a way of enhancing their development. In the view of Veenman *et al.* 'coaching can help teachers improve their instructional effectiveness by providing them with feedback on their functioning and stimulating them to be more reflective' (p. 321). However, a balance needs to be struck between 'the roles of mentor ("putting in") and coach ("pulling out")' (p. 324) with possibly mentoring appropriate for early stages of the induction programme and coaching for the later stages where the learner has more experience and confidence.

Coaching-mentoring

While many programmes make a careful distinction between mentoring and coaching, some programmes such as Veenman *et al.* (2001) see these as complementary. Thus Pask and Joy (2007, p. 246) write about the mentoring and coaching continuum, and argue that:

mentoring is the overarching concept, assembling accurately the picture of the 'present reality' and any tensions/points of focus as perceived by the client. But there would be little point in the exercise if the process stopped there. The point is not merely to analyse the present situation, but to change it! Coaching helps the client identify, plan and effect the changes s/he perceives to be necessary to realize the vision identified in the client's future.

For Pask and Joy (2007), then, the key is change in the practice and behaviour of the learner. While mentoring processes can support learning, it is the crucial link to changing and enhancing what a teacher/leader does that coaching can stimulate. Bloom *et al.* (2005) argue that their model of 'blended coaching strategies model' takes this process further: we need to move beyond just 'ways of doing' (p. 55), that is, the practices and actions of a professional, and look to the more fundamental process of 'ways of being' (p. 55), the sets of personal and interpersonal qualities, beliefs and values which shape practice (p. 55), in order to promote professional change. Thus coaches apply two core sets of strategies in a blended coaching model: instructional coaching and facilitative coaching. Instructional coaching is akin to mentoring and enables a learner to develop new knowledge or set of practices while facilitative coaching, more akin to classic coaching: '…enables the learner to learn *new ways* of being through observation, analysis, reinterpretation, and experimentation' (p. 56, emphasis in original).

Peer-supported learning
In each of the approaches explored above the crucial outcome is the enhancement of practice of the learner. Hobson (2003) noted benefits also for those taking on the mentor or coach role, including the fine tuning of skills, becoming clearer in the use of problem solving and enhancing strategies to reflect critically. Further, being a coach or mentor adds a sense of validation and confirmation of the professional's own practice. The possibilities of reciprocal learning have been captured in a number of peer-supported learning approaches. There are a range of terms used to describe peer-supported learning including 'co-mentoring' or 'co-coaching', 'mutual mentoring', 'collaborative coaching' and 'critical friends'. We will now explore some of the different approaches, including the use of peer mentoring, critical friends and peer coaching.

Peer mentoring

Teachers have frequently informally collaborated which has helped to develop their understanding and practice, and formal peer mentoring seeks to build on this. The strength of peer mentoring is the engendering of a sense of mutual support which enables teachers to explore their teaching with greater confidence. Some peer mentoring schemes are used as part of a wider programme of development in initial teacher education (Le Cornu, 2005). Other schemes of peer mentoring are concerned with support for minority groups such as peer mentoring among male primary teachers (Moore, 2009) or female academics (Driscoll *et al.*, 2009). In these examples, two people can mutually support each other in situations where there may be particular issues of access and equality. Although peer mentoring is less often used with highly experienced staff, here too, it can be found to be a powerful process of development and renewal (Smith, 2007). Oti (2009) indicates that peer mentoring should, like mentoring, be adequately resourced – without resourcing peer mentoring becomes just another burden. Further, formal schemes of peer mentoring cannot simply rely on existing good relationships and experience. Le Cornu (2005) demonstrates the importance of training in a scheme using a peer mentoring approach with student teachers and highlights the development of a mentoring attitude, interpersonal skills and critical reflection skills (p. 359) by both participants before a peer mentoring relationship can be entered into. Further, Smith (2007, p. 280) argues that peer mentoring must 'move beyond story-telling, networking, and socializing to a rigorous interaction focused on professional learning and development where the members challenge as well as support one another'. The skills of the peers in mentoring are important in order to ensure productive conversations. These studies point to the importance of purpose, structure and resourcing, and we find similar issues in the use of critical friends.

Critical friends

The idea of using 'critical friends' as a process of development in education was proposed by Stenhouse (1975), but it is only recently that this practice has become part of the repertoire of professional development activities. There seems to be a paradox built into the term 'critical friend', but as explained in a commonly used definition from Costa and Kallick (1993, p. 49), 'A critical friend … is a trusted person who asks provocative questions, provides data to be examined through another lens, and offers a critique of a person's work as a friend'. Critical friendships take a variety of forms. Swaffield's work (2004) points to the use of external critical friends as part of a whole-school improvement process, particularly a headteacher taking forward an improvement agenda. Another approach is the use of a critical friend to support an action research project in the classroom (Golby and Appleby, 1995). Other models are internally based, with staff acting as critical friends to each other. However, critical friends are not simply about 'friendships', but should provide another lens to raise critical questions to deal with some of the complex areas of education.

Dahlgren *et al.* (2006) investigated the use of critical friends as a means of developing reflection among medical educators where critical friends were used as a tool to promote self-knowledge and reflection. They argue for the role to 'be critical and to be a friend in equal proportions' (p. 73), to illuminate both strengths and weaknesses in professional practice. Here getting the balance between the ongoing familiar working relationship between teachers and the more interrogative activity in critical friendships is crucial. Farrell (2001) also provides an example of colleagues working together and observing. The data presented gives testimony to the need for critical friendship to develop over a period of time as trust and mutually understanding is built. Farrell also acknowledges that the process of critical friendship can be risky for individuals:

> Since critical friendships means self-disclosure and some process of change, the person who is reflecting should be in good personal psychological state in order to be able to confront any inconsistencies that may occur. It should be understood that reflection can cause doubt, and for that reason some people may not want to face any further uncertainties at this stage of life. So reflection is not for everyone. (p. 373)

Peer coaching

Peer or co-coaching is another approach designed to support change and improvement in classroom practice by providing feedback to each other. Based on their close study of peer coaching among experienced teachers, Zwart *et al.* (2007) argue that it must be part of an integrated approach which can embrace different aspects such as 'observation, reflection, exchanging professional ideas and shared problem solving' (p. 167). Peer coaching has been used in pre-service teacher education, where Lu (2010) suggests that peer coaching can enable student teachers to become active learners both as teachers and as coaches of their fellow student teachers. Used in schools, peer coaching has been found to strengthen collaborative practice, with Little (2005) arguing that peer coaching is a powerful means to support cooperative teaching situations and as well as building collaboration; peer coaching is potentially a valuable way of examining critically the process of teaching. However, one of the tensions evident in peer models of coaching, as with other peer-supported approaches, is the interrogatory stance. From the case study in medical education by Dahlgren *et al.* (2006), feedback between peers tended to be overwhelmingly positive. A similar trend is evident in peer coaching. The problematic place of feedback was questioned, particularly in a model of peer coaching developed by Showers and Joyce (1996). They found benefits for the teacher observing were often greater than for those being observed and receiving feedback. As a consequence, the programme was revised and the learning process became the act of observing another teacher and the reflective process this prompted on the observer's own practice. The use of feedback was subsequently omitted.

The examples of peer-supported learning discussed above largely relate to two practitioners working together, and this can have many benefits. However, while the approaches can build collaborative practice between two practitioners, these processes do not necessarily impact on the wider institutional context. There are examples of groups of practitioners working and learning collaboratively including the group coaching model from Showers and Joyce (1996). In this we can see traces of the use of professional learning communities where groups of staff collaborate to build their knowledge, understanding and classroom practice.

Professional learning communities

Professional learning communities (PLC) are becoming increasingly popular, promising the possibilities of school-based improvement as well as systems-wide development (Harris and Jones, 2010). Stoll *et al.* (2006) argue that professional learning communities 'hold considerable promise for capacity building for sustainable improvement' (p. 221). The emphasis here moves from individualised or dyadic experiences to more collaborative approaches. We see a variety of approaches in different contexts, with several plays on the term including teacher learning community, group learning teams, critical friendship groups and online networks. At the heart of these various approaches is a collaborative learning process designed to inform and improve practice.

Like other approaches discussed here, the antecedents of professional learning communities lie in ideas about the centrality of reflection and the importance of teacher engagement in the development of the school. Whereas in critical friendships there was an emphasis on sharing practice as part of a partnership, professional learning communities have a wider scope in fostering a culture of learning and development across a school. Vescio *et al.* (2008) argue that PLCs are informed by ideas from business and relate to the capacity of institutions to learn and enhance their development (Argyris and Schön, 1996).

Vescio *et al.* (2008) further argue that the use of collaborative learning groups is underpinned by two assumptions: first, that 'knowledge is situated in the day-to-day experience and is best understood through critical reflection with others who share the same experience' and second, by 'actively engaging in a professional learning community teachers will increase their professional knowledge and enhance student learning' (p. 81). In their survey of studies of professional learning community, Vescio *et al.* found evidence of impact on a teaching culture where strong norms were established through shared values evident in the PLC. Answers to the key question, however, concerning the impact on pupil learning, were less evident. In Supovitz's (2002) four-year evaluation, cultural change was evident in PLCs, but the higher levels of interaction and collaboration did not necessarily bring about a greater concentration of the practice of teaching. He points to professional learning communities needing to embrace different collaborative activities where there is a clear focus on teaching and learning. This approach is evident in Snow-Gerono's (2005) study of the use of an inquiry-based approach to learning. She argues that professional learning communities can establish as normative, practices that in everyday school life might be avoided; with professional learning communities 'providing opportunities for dialogue which also made it safe to ask questions and work in a community where uncertainty was not only valued but supported' (p. 242). It is these elements of dialogue, questioning and critical enquiry that are central to the effective use of the range of approaches explored in this book.

Developing knowledge and criticality

As in other professions, in approaches to learning for both novice and experienced practitioners in education, a high value is placed on forms of experiential learning which enable practitioners to grapple with the day-to-day realities of the context in which they practice as a professional. This focus on enhancing practice is a necessary element where teacher learning has to relate to their practice in the classroom or school and the learning needs of pupils. Thus we have seen experiential pedagogies such as mentoring, coaching, peer-supported learning come increasingly to the fore. Learning with, and from, peers in the form of 'learning communities' has also become an important development process, both for the individual practitioners and for the school as a community. The experiential pedagogies explored here are each a powerful means of engaging in reflective practice, particularly around issues of personal qualities and commitments and interpersonal skills which are important in the development of professional actions. However, these are not the only dimensions of professional practice we need to consider. While accepting that both teaching and leadership in education are social processes, these are much more complex processes than simply interacting with others. This interaction has to be purposeful, ethically sound and result in educational benefits to the learner. We have to be careful and ensure that teacher learning does not become reductive, focusing largely on narrow areas of routine practice. Therefore exploration of experiences, personal skills and attributes needs to be balanced by the development of deeper understandings of significant areas in learning and teaching, and in leadership, particularly given the rapidly expanding knowledge base of these areas.

In Scotland we have a suite of professional standards which run from initial teacher education to headship:

- The Standard for Initial Teacher Education (GTCS, 2006a)
- The Standard for Full Registration (GTCS, 2006b)
- The Standard for Chartered Teacher (GTCS, 2009)
- The Standard for Headship (SEED, 2005a)

The underpinning construction of professional practice across these standards is based on the idea of reflective practice. If we are to see teaching as a theoretically informed practice we have to appreciate that it is also a deeply contested process where there are not simple, routine solutions notwithstanding the waves of policies which suggest that it is. There is an increasing emphasis developing and sustaining an interrogatory approach that fosters innovation and enhancement of professional practice. In each standard there is the clear link made between practice in the form of 'professional actions' and values and personal commitment as well as knowledge and understanding. For example, in the professional standard to be met by every teacher in Scotland, the Standard for Full Registration (GTCS 2006b, pp. 7–9), teachers are expected to have knowledge and understanding of the curriculum including cross-curricular themes and the nature of the curriculum and its development, and these understandings must be demonstrated in their planning of programmes. In addition, all teachers are expected to have an understanding of the educational system, policy and practice and to be able set out their professional values based on theoretical principles including research-based knowledge of learning and teaching.

Reflection is a critical component of professional practice (Schon 1983, Brookfield 1995), but this reflection is not simply contemplation or superficial evaluation. Instead, reflection has to be purposeful, rigorous and take on a critical dimension in order to bring about change. The process of reflection rests on asking probing questions based on theoretically sound principles in order to reform and improve practice. Therefore, in this discussion of experiential pedagogies we have to consider the complementarity of these pedagogic approaches with other pedagogies to be found in professional learning that can support the development of theoretical and critical perspectives, particularly tutoring and facilitation.

Tutoring and facilitation

Traditions of course-based provision for initial and continuing professional development particularly award-bearing programmes have been criticised historically for focusing almost exclusively on theory and knowledge building (Schon, 1983). However, in Scotland a range of programmes have been developed which combine structured experiential learning through mentoring, coaching and peer-supported learning with knowledge building and the development of criticality. Therefore, we cannot lose sight of other pedagogies that have a crucial place in professional learning, particularly tutoring and facilitation which relate more to the development of knowledge and understanding. The terms 'tutoring' and 'facilitation' tend to be used interchangeably, but there are some distinctions we can draw.

In tertiary and professional education tutoring is more commonly associated with the development of knowledge and understanding and so relies on expertise. In tutoring there is a clear didactic process where a tutor seeks to develop knowledge and understanding and to some degree, skill. Therefore the tutor has to have expertise in the particular area. However, the role of tutoring is not solely about 'imparting knowledge'. Tutoring like the other pedagogies is an interactive process between tutor and learner, but the focus is on knowledge and understanding. Chi *et al.* (2001) identify some of the processes of tutoring which include questioning and feedback. These are approaches evident in experiential pedagogies, but in tutoring there is also the use of input, explanations, discussion and scaffolding. The expertise of the tutor in the particular area of knowledge come through each aspect of the process of scaffolding, through the design of curricula, tasks set individuals and groups, and through interaction where building knowledge is developed through explanation and questioning.

Tutoring has an instructional dimension concerned with the content of learning, which stands in contrast to facilitation which is less about conveying knowledge and more about fostering learning through social constructivist processes. Thus the task of the facilitator is to ensure full participation, guiding groups to build collaborative learning practices, using questioning and reflection to enable learners plan and reflect on their learning. However, this is not a 'content-free' process.

Facilitation is a pedagogy that has become increasingly evident in tertiary and professional education, particularly medical education, which is designed on the basis of problem-based learning (PBL). PBL is based on collaborative group learning where learners work through problems or scenarios researching issues, gathering information on which to base diagnosis and treatment. In this the co-constructivist approach to learning is clearly evident, but the crucial aspect is not just a process of reflection on experience but the seeking and using of a range of sources of knowledge including theoretical and research-based knowledge in order to ground learning and practice in a sound theoretical frame. Part of the facilitation process is to guide learners to these sources of knowledge, and so there is an assumption that the facilitator has the prerequisite knowledge (McLean, 2003). There is considerable debate in PBL about the tension between the expertise of the tutor and the facilitation of learning, with an emphasis, on the one hand, on the importance of developing a theoretically sound understanding, and, on the other hand, on fostering the independence of the learner. However, as Neville (1999, p. 393) proposes:

> the role dichotomy between process facilitator and content resource may be more apparent than real and that there is evidence pointing towards a consideration of a balanced interaction of these functions as the optimal tutor role.

Conclusion

Given the emphasis on expertise in both the roles of tutoring and facilitation, there is a question than about whether these pedagogies can only be used by 'experts' such as academics or researchers. Again, we should be wary of such assumptions, partly because this perpetuates a perceived divide between theory and practice. There has to be a concern about accessing up-to-date knowledge and theoretically sound principles; tutoring and facilitation have much to offer here, but these should be part of a 'mixed economy' (Gronn *et al.* 2009) where different pedagogies complement one another. This idea of an optimal role suggests that there is not one particular pedagogy that holds the key to effective professional learning, but, instead, the optimum is to draw from a range of pedagogies in the design and delivery of professional learning opportunities. Thus in Chapters 3 and 4 both Martin and Torrance discuss professional learning programmes which combine experiential pedagogies such as mentoring, coaching or critical friends with the more knowledge-focused pedagogies of tutoring and facilitation. Further, in some forms of peer-supported learning particularly professional learning communities, as Carroll argues in Chapter 5, sharing and reflecting on practice and experience is centred on investigative learning methodologies where teachers draw on theoretical and research-based material to interrogate, trial and reform their practice as leaders, thus generating contextualised bodies of knowledge about learning and teaching within their own setting.

CHAPTER 3

Preparing to teach: an examination of mentoring in the Scottish teacher induction scheme

Margaret Martin

Introduction

One of the most common contexts for mentoring in education in different national systems is the induction of new teachers. As part of the teacher induction scheme introduced in Scotland in 2002 (SEED, 2001), newly qualified teachers became entitled to a range of support mechanisms, including access to a mentor during their first year of teaching. In line then with many other countries (Asia-Pacific Economic Cooperation Ministerial Group, 1997; American Confederation of Teachers, 2001), Scotland has moved to a more structured induction process for new teachers as they enter the profession, and mentoring is a key component of the scheme. In this chapter the nature and scope of the mentoring offered to new teachers and its possible impact is explored, as well as alternative approaches for the development of beginning teachers. The focus will therefore be on answering the following key questions:

- What is the nature and scope of mentoring of new teachers?
- What effect does the experience of mentoring appear to have on the professional development of new teachers?
- How might alternative conceptualisations of the mentoring component of induction process lead to different outcomes?

Nature and scope of mentoring of new teachers

In Scotland, as in many other countries, the induction scheme is largely operational, focusing the processes by which the newly qualified teacher will achieve the Standard for Full Registration (GTCS, 2006b). The

Scheme offers newly qualified teachers (NQTs) a reduced class commitment (originally 0.7 full-time equivalent but currently – 2011 – the subject of negotiation), dedicated time set aside for professional development, and access to an experienced teacher or teachers who will act as supporters or mentors during the year (GTCS 2011a). There are no wider purposes stated in relation to the Induction Scheme. The advice on the GTCS website (2011b) relates almost entirely to the technical processes involved and how to navigate your way through them. It is instead implicitly understood that induction is an important part of teacher education and other education systems across the UK now have teacher induction schemes. Although England, Scotland and Wales all have formal induction schemes in place, there are some variations in the regulations and amount of support. Bubb (2007, p. 28) describes the responsibilities of the induction tutor as follows:

- making sure that NQTs know and understand the roles and responsibilities of everyone in induction;
- organising, in consultation with the NQTs, a tailored programme of monitoring, support and assessment;
- co-ordinating and carrying out lesson observations and the follow up discussions;
- reviewing progress against objectives and core standards;
- ensuring that dated records are kept of the monitoring, support, and formative and summative assessment activities.

While she is describing the English system, this list of responsibilities would be similar in other UK countries. The emphasis is on support in order to prove competence and meet standards. This emphasis on support rather than 'testing' highlights the key developmental aspect of induction, but there is also the process of socialisation into the teaching profession. Thus, Hurling-Austin (1990) offers five common goals for teacher induction programmes based on a review of the literature:

- to improve teaching performance;
- to increase the retention of promising beginning teachers during the induction years;
- to promote the personal and professional well-being of beginning teachers by improving teachers' attitudes towards themselves and the profession;
- to satisfy mandated requirements related to induction and certification;

- to transmit the culture of the system to beginning teachers. (cited by Cullingford, 2006, p. 39)

O'Brien and Draper (2006, p. 7) suggest a broad understanding of the notion of induction would include socialisation, organisational familiarisation and sensitisation, developmental support and scope for contribution. Socialisation and the transmission of culture are of most interest in this critique of current practice in relation to mentoring as a key component of the induction of new teachers, since they are rarely stated as intended outcomes of formal schemes. The implicit aims, which are so strongly influenced by context, need to be made explicit and then subjected to scrutiny. The mentoring process is not value-free and yet it is often characterised as such, focusing mainly on a fairly benign support of the new teacher into the profession and the assessment of the development of teaching skills in the classroom. In this chapter the aim is to explore the underlying effects of a system which aims to produce one set of outcomes, but may, inadvertently or otherwise, in fact produce another.

Definitions of mentoring have been offered in previous chapters, and these are useful in considering the professional development of new teachers. Historically, the central factor in mentoring is the acknowledgement of the experience, wisdom and craft knowledge of the mentor, and it can therefore be construed as a model of learning where the apprentice or novice learns at the feet of the expert (Strong, 2009). This model is not unproblematic. It can be characterised as a deficit model where the new teacher is effectively an empty vessel waiting to be filled by the experienced practitioner. It can lead to a search for security and identity as 'expert' on the part of the new teacher, and in this way the mentoring process may actually narrow the conception of good teacher as it becomes tied up in the practice and values of one particular practitioner. Forde in Chapter 2 has alluded to the dangers of encouraging this kind of conformity and the potential for groupthink and lack of scrutiny of existing practice. It can be no more relevant than to beginning teachers, keen to meet expectations. Achinstein (2006, p. 123) warns of the possibility that 'New teachers' beliefs and actions may conflict with existing organisational norms and they may face issues of power, interest and negotiation.' The role of the mentor cast as 'expert' is not necessarily going to be conducive to the development of a critical stance in the 'novice' teacher. Therefore, the role and skills of the mentor are worthy of investigation. Portner (2008) argues that a mentor role includes the following four functions:

- *Relating* involves building and maintaining relationships based on mutual trust, respect and professionalism.
- *Assessing* involves gathering and diagnosing data about the mentees teaching and learning to determine competence.
- *Coaching* involves asking the right questions, at the right time and in the right way to encourage mentees to reflect on their decisions.
- *Guiding* behaviours stimulate critical and creative thinking.

While there is much self-reported evidence that the first three of these roles are helpful to the new teacher, the last of these functions needs to be explored, particularly in relation to 'critical thinking'. In socialising new teachers into the school system, it can be argued that mentors may in fact be stifling the very critical thinking being advocated above and encourage a compliance with, and acceptance of, the status quo in order to 'fit in'.

The role of the mentor and the content and conduct of the mentoring will, of course, be determined by the stated outcomes expected to be achieved and for which the mentor may be held accountable at the end of the induction period. Where the requirement to meet standards to gain qualifications is involved, meeting the needs of the system may take precedence. The paperwork and form filling involved in the induction scheme is an aspect of the procedure which mentors take very seriously. In Scotland, this paperwork is submitted to the GTCS at the end of the probationary period as evidence of the new teacher's progress during the first year. It is common therefore for mentors to become focused on the procedures rather than the learning process. There are high stakes involved for the new teacher, as full registration is dependent upon successful completion of the reports from the school, and there are also high stakes involved for the mentor in being seen to carry out their duties as laid down by the scheme. It is therefore not surprising that the focus of the mentoring can become narrowed to that which is assessed and that a wider perspective of the nature outlined above is often not on the agenda – either for the new teacher or the school.

While this paperwork is important, it cannot be the main focus of mentoring process in induction, since it is so likely to encourage conformity. Devos (2010, p. 1222) warns that the emphasis focuses on 'How?' rather than 'What' or 'Why?', and that the 'relationship is driven by the documentation and the demands of full registration, which in turn are framed through the discourses of professional standards'. New teachers report a strong sense of the pressure to conform. As one commented, 'One may fall into the bad habits of the mentor without an outside assessment to monitor progress' (Rippon and Martin, 2003, p. 1). The apprenticeship model assumes there is one way to operate and it is the best way. This has been partially blamed for the teaching profession's inability to enact change and regenerate itself (Tickle, 2000). It is a model of teacher education which does not always facilitate diversity in teaching styles and approaches to develop according to individual strengths and interests. Probationer teachers could be compelled to conform to the dominant model of teaching to ensure their fully registered place in the profession. Given the power dimension to the supporter–probationer relationship, it is not surprising one student teacher suggested: 'for me the first year is about conforming to the school ethos' (Rippon and Martin, 2003, p. 16).

It would seem, therefore, that the practices of the mentoring relationship may be intrinsically linked to the aspects of induction for which schools and local authorities are held publicly accountable. If the purpose is to meet a standard, as is the case in the different systems in the UK, then that high stakes requirement is the one which will be supported. This approach may need to be reviewed if new teachers are to be supported in developing their own sense of values, the actions that relate to them and the tensions these values in action might present in the school context. Before moving to explore the alternatives, we will examine the experiences of new teachers in order to assess the impact of mentoring on their professional development.

What effect does the experience of mentoring have on new teachers?
There is a strong sense in education that mentoring is a 'good thing', and it is not surprising that, for many new teachers, the allocation of an experienced support person results in positive self-reporting of the experience (Devos, 2010). There is a wide range of evidence from diverse sources to support the assertion that, in general terms, new teachers are positively affected by the mentoring process. Hobson *et al.* (2009) argue that beginning teacher mentoring has great potential, and outline some of the reported benefits: emotional and psychological support, increasing confidence, support with classroom management and handling behaviour, and socialisation into the profession. However, they also point to the fact that this potential is often unrealised because of the variation in

the nature and quality of support, the lack of challenge, and insufficient attention to pedagogical issues, the promotion of reflective practice and social justice issues. They argue that this transmission model promotes conventional practices and means that new teachers are unlikely to challenge the status quo in schools. Strong (2009) examines the effect of induction programmes in the USA, and while reporting that almost all the research indicates a positive experience for teachers, also questions the extent to which claims can be made with regard to a direct effect on teaching performance.

Alongside this generally positive self-reporting, new teachers often emphasise the particular importance of the professional relationship which they develop with the mentor, and the personal attributes and dispositions which are conducive to a positive mentoring experience (Martin and Rippon, 2003). There is no doubt that, in terms of pastoral support, many mentors would seem to have a great deal to offer new teachers as they move into their professional role. There is a strong sense of the way in which this kind of personal support aids new teachers in settling in to their new context and role. Ehrich *et al.* (2002) identify a range of positive outcomes for mentees in their review of research:

- support/ empathy/ encouragement/counselling/friendship;
- help with teaching strategies/ subject knowledge/ resources;
- discussion/sharing ideas/ problems/ advice from peers;
- feedback/ positive reinforcement;
- increased self-confidence;
- career affirmation/commitment.

HMIe (2005) found that new teachers in Scotland were generally well supported and the overall mentoring was having a positive effect on the development of new teachers.

While this can be seen as a very positive set of circumstances, there are issues here, which we have already raised, around reproduction of the status quo, particularly in relation to values and beliefs and school culture. This would point to the need for a critical analysis of the mentor's gate-keeping role and their part in shaping the identity of new teachers. It has been suggested that the power of assessment could escalate the trend for teachers to socialise new recruits into becoming mirror images of themselves in an apprenticeship model of training teachers (Bleach, 2001). Probationer teachers could be compelled to conform to the dominant model of teaching to ensure their fully registered place in the profession. Smith

(2001, p. 314) has suggested that most teacher mentors have a 'strong sense of the sort of person who should or should not be allowed to become a teacher'. Interestingly, in a study by Rippon and Martin (2003) one NQT referred to the induction supporter as a 'probation officer', someone who would be out to control their behaviours and practices in line with the culture of the school.

Furthermore, positive experiences of the mentoring relationship are not universal, and there are difficulties associated with the complexities of this process. Hobson *et al.* (2009) argue that the necessary conditions do not always exist and the contextual support so valued by new teachers is often variable. Not all new teachers find they are matched with a supportive mentor who eases their transition into the profession. Long (2009) points to the difficulties associated with the skills and disposition of the mentor, the training provided for them, the time allocation and the amount and quality of feedback. Draper and O'Brien (2006, p. 1) also highlight that

> studies of induction reveal there are real differences in teacher experiences and especially in teacher experiences in the early time in a new post. For many, there is a greater likelihood of early difficulties rather than early successes being experienced.

In short, the structures are not always effective and policy does not ensure quality practice.

For the mentor some of the same issues arise. Many mentors report the professional satisfaction they experience when mentoring new teachers and this is well documented. Ehrich *et al.* (2002) reported the following positive outcomes for mentors:

- collegiality/ collaboration/ networking/ sharing ideas/ knowledge;
- reflection;
- professional development;
- personal satisfaction/ reward/growth;
- interpersonal skill development;
- enjoyment/ stimulation/ challenge.

However, mentors also experience difficulties as they try to carry out this important role: for example, lack of sufficient training, lack of sufficient time, the tensions in being supporter and assessor. The importance of mentor selection, training, preparation and a well-thought-through mentoring strategy cannot be overemphasised. The demands on the induction supporter are immense. There is a need for systematic training for induction supporters and probationer teachers which goes beyond consideration of the procedural arrangements. Staff development opportunities have to include deliberation of the personal and power relationships at work.

Even where there is acknowledgement of the positive impact that there can be as a result of the development of the mentor–mentee relationship, there are still questions around the possible difficulties that can arise, for both parties. These should not be underestimated, and can be set alongside the facts that the positive impacts outlined above are mostly based on self-reporting and that there is little hard evidence of the impact of mentoring on the effectiveness of teachers or the quality of learning in the classroom. It seems therefore that, while there are some clearly identified and mainly self-reported benefits from the mentoring of new teachers, there are many unresolved issues in relation to the outcomes. Perhaps we need to look at the problem differently.

How might alternative conceptualisations of the mentoring component of the induction process lead to different outcomes?

While there are many possible benefits to new teachers in learning alongside experienced practitioners, it can be argued that a much broader conception of the notion of mentoring is required if we are to prepare new teachers to take on the role of professional educator for the twenty-first century. This would involve a more autonomous model of learning where the learner would be required to be more critically reflective. In this model of mentoring, teachers would develop a research disposition, including the ability to theorise and interpret, explain and judge experience, and the development of an understanding of critical reflection is therefore crucial. It would also encourage the development of micro political awareness, so important in understanding school politics and the resulting conflicts that can arise, as well as macro political awareness in order to understand the impact of external influences on the work of schools.

This wider view of the induction process and the place of mentoring within it is supported in the literature by a number of different authors (Cullingford, 2006; Devos, 2010; Long, 2009) and the arguments for taking a broader perspective are related to the need to move away from a narrow focus almost exclusively on the technical and instrumental aspects of practice to a wider notion of the development of teacher identity and purpose. The literature also leads us to consider the argument that the current approach encourages new teachers to conform to the system and to become uncritically accepting of the status quo. From this position, it is therefore argued that the wider world of education outwith the classroom needs to be included as an integral part of the induction process, developing the social and political awareness of new teachers as they enter the profession. Achinstein (2006) argues for the development of political literacy in new teachers: that is, the facility to scrutinise and interrogate the policies and practices of the school, the local authority and government in relation to education. Kelchtermans and Ballet (2002) found that new teachers are rarely aware of the macro or micro politics of schools and schooling and therefore ill- equipped to deal with the possible tensions and conflicts which arise as a result. The ability to understand and reflect critically upon the context within which they work is unlikely to be developed if mentoring is seen only as a mechanism for learning about the mechanics and technicalities of teaching and for proving competence.

If the mentoring process as part of the induction of new teachers is indeed still a work in progress in terms of its impact on schools and teachers, perhaps it is time to consider new ways of looking at induction and the mentoring which has become such an integral part of it. This involves a deeper examination of the purposes of new teacher induction, the principles which might underpin the process, and the policies and practices which flow from those principles. It seems that a fairly radical shift is required in the thinking of those who are responsible for induction schemes if the broader perspective advocated here is to have any impact on the practices of mentoring and the outcomes of induction. So what might an alternative approach look like?

Firstly, the values and beliefs that inform the induction process need to be made explicit and subjected to scrutiny. There is little evidence in most induction schemes that the aims relate to much beyond operational or technical assistance with meeting standards, teaching practice and pastoral integration into the life of the school. There is reference to the development of various forms of reflective practice, but little about any engagement with school and government policy. It is difficult to find reference to the development of political literacy, whether at micro or macro level, and indeed in the most recent HMIe evaluation of induction in Scotland (SEED 2008) these matters are barely mentioned. The implication is that what is measured, assessed and evaluated in teacher induction relates to the narrow focus on craft knowledge, the completion of appropriate documentation and, to a certain extent, the quality of the mentoring relationship. There is an emphasis on evaluating performance and proving competence. There is an absence of focus on values, underlying philosophy and the principles upon which the development of beginning teachers is being built. In the absence of such a foundation, it is easy to see how the operational and mechanistic focus can become central.

Secondly, the social and political awareness of teachers needs to move up the agenda. Understanding 'the bigger picture' within which they operate is an important dimension of a new teacher's development. Initial teacher education programmes are often criticised for a lack of focus on this bigger picture thinking and the development of a critical professional stance (McMahon *et al.*, 2011). In postgraduate school leadership development programmes this has become a central concern and an obvious gap in the knowledge and understanding of many candidates. This may be related to the fact that many teachers often move through the education system to teaching, without ever leaving it to operate in the 'outside world', and therefore may be less likely to criticise it, or because those who end up in teaching have generally been successful in school, conformed to the system and possibly not had much cause to become politicised. It can be argued then that this is an area worthy of greater exploration in the professional development of teachers.

It is, however, not always easy to persuade teachers of the need to take a wider view of their work, although it can be argued that it is an essential element of their development. Important insights, derived from consideration of identity, values and purposes of education, should inform practice and focus attention on the 'Why?' rather than just the 'How?' of teaching. This approach encourages new teachers to ask important questions about the rationale that underpins their professional practice and subject their everyday professional actions to critical scrutiny. Such scrutiny allows teachers to develop a professional stance based on critical reflection rather than 'unexamined common sense', as Brookfield (1995) argues. He advocates the use of four lenses through which to view what we do from different angles to examine our underlying assumptions: our autobiographies as learners and teachers, the views of colleagues, student feedback and, importantly, related literature. He asks us to step outside ourselves to examine how some of our deeply held values and beliefs are informing our practice.

Making decisions about the kind of teacher you are going to be is central to the development of the identity and integrity of new professionals. This involves consideration of the purposes of education in the global arena of the twenty-first century and teachers' perceptions of their place in delivering those purposes in their everyday work in schools. These are contested areas, and there are controversial issues about which new teachers need to develop an informed view. This wider context, therefore, is worthy of deeper exploration.

In addition, new teachers are often unprepared for the school-level politics and experience what has been described by Kelchtermans and Ballet (2002) as 'praxis shock'. It would therefore be important for them to develop micro political literacy, including the skills to understand and handle school-level conflict, as well as macro political awareness and the ability to articulate their own professional values. This gap in skill became obvious in the experience of new teachers encountering the school context as an employee for the first time, as reported by Rippon and Martin (2006) in their study of probationer teachers entering the system. Achinstein (2006) writes about the need for new teachers to learn how to 'read' the school context and develop the political knowledge and skill to advocate for themselves, as well as the challenges faced by mentors in guiding new teachers to help them articulate their own values.

Thirdly, the development and support of new teachers could be enhanced by a community or team approach to mentoring, rather than the traditional top–down model. Carroll in Chapter 5 looks at professional learning communities in greater depth but here we can consider how a more collaborative approach might benefit probationary teachers and augment the dyadic mentoring relationship. A professional learning community (PLC) is way of working in a school – a set of relationships and structures designed to encourage real collaboration by staff to ensure improvement in pupil learning (Hord, 2004; DuFour *et al.*, 2006; Huffman and Hipp, 2003). Teacher learning is at the heart of a professional learning community; while teaching has traditionally been a fairly isolated activity, this approach encourages working together with colleagues with the express purpose of sharing expertise and stimulating debate and discussion about approaches to teaching and learning. This mutual examination of practice provides the opportunity for structured conversations about learning which help teachers to make sense of the new ideas they are experimenting with by sharing their success and failures. In a learning community, a different approach is taken, where the need for particular areas to be developed are identified through enquiry and evaluation. To be effective in a PLC, enquiry into pupil learning is not done in isolation, but as part of a collaborative endeavour. The place here for professional development of new teachers is clear.

Such a collaborative model of school learning would allow new teachers to benefit from the experience and insight of a range of staff in the school, but would also create the conditions where new teachers could make their own valid contribution to the collective learning in the school. Many new teachers leave initial teacher education (ITE) with a wide range of up-to-date skills and knowledge from which their colleagues could and should benefit. This approach embeds new teachers' development in the professional learning of the school and takes us away from what could be argued is a deficit model of the 'novice' teacher. Clearly, this way of working with new teachers in underpinned by a different philosophy and involves a shift in the traditional power relationships in the school. Context is therefore key, and the structural, social and cultural factors at play will determine the extent to which new teachers can be afforded a different kind of professional development. This would be based on a collaborative mentoring arrangement where mutually beneficial learning is enabled through the formal and informal interactions with peers as part of a professional learning community. This approach allows new teachers to see their professional learning as an integral part of the school culture and not a 'one-off' induction experience. Long (2009) argues convincingly for this way of working as part of the school's wider professional learning networks, rather than a stand-alone programme for new teachers, with the aim of blurring the lines between 'expert' and 'novice' teachers. It encourages them to think in terms of a continuum of ongoing professional learning based on developing the habit of inquiring into their own practice and making sense of the outcomes with colleagues.

And lastly, a different conception of the mentor role would be characterised by a stronger emphasis on developing criticality, independence and the individual identity of the mentee. The involves a different set of skills and dispositions on the part of the mentor which are not routinely developed as part of most induction schemes and which require a greater degree of social and political awareness and the wider policy context and the implications for new teachers as they develop their own professional stance. Achinstein (2006) argues that the mentor should become more of a 'critical change agent' rather than a 'local guide'. These are much more sophisticated requirements of the mentor and not necessarily seen by them, the school or the local authority, as the most important dimension of their role. The focus on critical reflection and subjecting assumptions to scrutiny would encourage new teachers to develop a research disposition, including the ability to theorise, interpret, explain and judge experience.

CHAPTER 4

Preparing to lead: coaching, mentoring and tutoring in leadership development

Deirdre Torrance

Introduction

Internationally, leadership has become a key policy theme, with attention focused on supporting the professional development of the next generation of school leaders. Despite the considerable energies and funding invested in school leadership preparation, there is still much to be learned in relation to how best to support professional development in this area. In Scotland, the search continues for effective experiential approaches to support adult learning. Coaching has gained prominence in recent years and has been positioned as a desirable element of leadership preparation. This chapter begins with a review of developments leading to this point, to inform understandings of such positioning. Through a discussion of traditional and alternative models of leadership and, more specifically, headship preparation programmes, emerging themes are explored. Given all that we have come to understand about leadership preparation, key considerations are discussed in relation to experiential approaches and their impact on learners, with a specific focus on coaching and mentoring.

Leadership development: the background

Leadership development is high on the agenda. Ten years on from the introduction of the *Teaching Profession for the 21st Century* (TP21) (SEED, 2001), school leadership is conceived as 'both individual and shared' (HMIe, 2006, p. 93), and located at all levels of the school organisation

(Educational Institute for Scotland [EIS], 2010; GTCS, 2010; HMIe, 2007, p. 16; HMIe, 2010). In parallel with this view, the leadership of the head-teacher has been specifically linked with school improvement (Woods *et al.*, 2007) and is still recognised as playing a key role, being 'ultimately accountable' for the work of the school. That dual discourse is reflected within the Standard for Headship (SEED, 2005a), in which responsibility for staff engagement in school improvement processes ultimately rests with the headteacher.

Identifying and developing school leaders has become an imperative within an apparent global headteacher recruitment and retention crisis (Bush, 2008; Rhodes and Brundrett, 2010). As school governance became further devolved, the role of the headteacher became increasingly chal-lenging, losing appeal faced with multiple, competing and conflicting accountabilities. TP21 (SEED, 2001), through its resulting flatter man-agement structures (MacBeath *et al.*, 2009, pp. 33, 49), impacted nega-tively on the workload and 'professional latitude' of headteachers as well as inadvertently creating a number of disincentives to promotion, putting a 'spanner in the works of career progression' for aspirants. As a result, relatively small numbers sought and completed professional development opportunities afforded by programmes leading to the Scottish Qualifica-tion for Headship (SQH).

In keeping with the development of a distributed perspective on lead-ership, whilst recognising that 'the capacities of headteachers need to be supported and developed' through key stages in a teacher's career (Woods *et al.*, 2007, p. 7), the then Scottish Executive (SEED, p. 2003) set out a framework for educational leadership: project leadership; team leadership; school leadership; strategic leadership. However, perhaps as a pragmatic response to the perceived headteacher recruitment crisis and focus on suc-cession planning (Hanbury, 2009), until very recently efforts continued to be focused mainly on preparation for headship.

Pre-1990, leadership development was, in the main, concerned with the development needs of serving headteachers. Post-1990 leadership development has increasingly focused more on leadership rather than on management, and has become increasingly preoccupied with developing organisational leadership capacity building, in tandem with the develop-ment of individuals' leadership confidence and competence. Far greater emphasis has been placed on personal transformation through the use of experiential and peer-supported methodologies such as coaching and mentoring in more recently developed government-sponsored leadership preparation programmes (SEED, 2005b), with a potential overemphasis on behaviours and emotions. This, despite the caution Forde highlights in Chapter 2, in relation to the dangers inherent when personal development is emphasised at the expense of intellectual development. Discussion as to what constitutes effective leadership preparation is interlinked with such policy objectives.

The inception of the Scottish Qualification for Headship (SQH)

The programme leading to the award of the SQH was designed in accordance with the Standard for Headship (SfH) (SEED, 2005a) setting out the key aspects of professionalism and expertise that the Scottish education system requires of those who are entrusted with the leadership and management of its schools. The SfH serves as the template against which those aspiring to headship may be assessed in order to determine their strengths and areas for professional development. The challenge was to design and deliver programmes addressing the professional needs of teachers whilst maintaining academic rigour (Black *et al.*, 1994). This prompted the development of Masters' programmes in education that blended formalised provision with professional experience, individualised development and academic qualification (Brundrett, 2010; Davies and Ellison, 1994).

Each leadership preparation model comprises benefits and shortcomings. The key is to harness the best of each and guard against the worst. How best to do so, however, is a complex matter (Brundrett and Crawford, 2008; Bush, 2008; Forde, 2011). The SQH was designed around a set of design principles (Reeves *et al.*, 2002) underpinned by research into professional learning (for example, Argyris, 1976; Earl and Katz, 2002; Eraut, 1994; Kolb, 1984; Schön, 1987), emphasising 'process knowledge' achieved in the fullness of time through critical reflection on, in and for practice, drawing from external perspectives and continuous formative feedback to facilitate learning, leading to influence on practice in order to make a real difference in schools. The learning and assessment activities were designed to make connections between the personal and professional context of the individual, the policy context in Scotland and the conceptual and research framework written up in the international literature on school leadership and management, and professional development. The emphasis on partnership arrangements between employers and university providers (O'Brien and Draper, 2001) enabled colleagues to work in a unique manner to oversee, develop and deliver the programme to situate current Scottish practice in a broader literature and academic framework (O'Brien and Torrance, 2006), maintaining a balance between the theoretical and the practical, the professional and the academic, the school context and the structured development afforded by the programme (Cowie, 2008).

Tutoring, mentoring and coaching within the design of the SQH

The SQH concept was relatively unique in that, on completion, participants were awarded the SQH by the Scottish Government, in addition to the PG Diploma by a university. This led to intensive professional development, within a blended learning approach (Forde, 2011), necessitating significantly higher levels of support than standard postgraduate programmes of study. That support involved tutoring and mentoring, and to a lesser degree coaching, provided by university tutors, practising headteacher supporters and headteacher field assessors. Support is provided 'in the round', impacting on leadership practice and school effectiveness, through emphaseses on the central importance of the headteacher (Brundrett, 2010). Indeed, the school context is 'a vital consideration where the school is used as the site for learning' (Reeves *et al.*, 2002), raising both practical and ethical considerations (Cowie, 2005). The headteacher mentor role requires a critical friend approach as well as a gatekeeper role for opportunities to lead and manage at whole-school level.

The programme leading to the SQH was positively evaluated (Menter *et al.*, 2003) and highly regarded (OECD, 2007). The main criticisms levelled at it related to a perceived tension between academic and practice components, its intensity of workload and the 'extended' 26-month completion period. Against the backdrop of a perceived headteacher recruitment crisis (Hanbury, 2009), the emphasis on leadership and its distributed perspective in the policy discourse with a prerequisite of well-developed personal qualities and interpersonal skills (Robertson, 2009; Slater, 2008), as well as an anti-academic view by a body of influential policy shapers intent on positioning coaching and mentoring as an alternative to supporting the professional development needs of a perceived untapped group of depute headteachers, the ground was fertile for the development of an alternative headteacher preparation programme.

The privileged position of coaching and mentoring in headteacher preparation

Coaching and mentoring in teacher CPD gained popularity at a remarkable pace across Scotland. Since 2004, mentoring became favoured in teacher preparation through the implementation of a national mentoring scheme for the induction of newly qualified teachers. In 2005, coaching and mentoring projects were developed across 32 local authorities arising from *Leadership: A Discussion Paper* (SEED, 2005b), with national investment of Scottish Executive money reported to be in the region of £4m. Experiential learning was privileged above intellectual development. Amongst the government themes, or 'specific SEED interest/proposals' explored at that time, was to consider developing a pilot programme 'Head Teacher as Coach' as well as 'coaching for headship (supporting HT development)' (Finnie, 2005, p. 2).

Two key government priorities coalesced: the drive to address a perceived headteacher recruitment crisis, through coaching aspirant heads. Coaching was constructed as holding the key for personal transformation in leadership development, to instil self-confidence and validation of professional capability, to assist individuals to identify how their practice should improve and to provide the space to explore how best to do so. However, there were a number of issues not grappled with in this policy in relation to purposes, definitions and use:

- the implications of adopting business models focusing on weaknesses to be improved and constituting the stage before underperformance measures (as in the approach advocated by Fournies, 2000);
- the lack of consensus as to the distinctiveness of coaching as compared to mentoring, or as to an agreed definition for coaching (Hanbury, 2009; Ives, 2008) was not considered;
- the scant research into coaching for leadership development (Blackman, 2010) and lack of evidence of coaching impact (Davidson *et al.*, 2008, p. 4; Hartley and Hinksman, 2003; Jackson, 2005), resulting in 'the jury of the research community [being] still out'.

The coaching model broadly endorsed by the national CPD team to be adopted across Scotland was based on the GROW model (Whitmore, 2002) with its sequence of goals, reality, options and will, impacting on action and performance (as discussed by Forde in Chapter 2). A 'blended coaching' (Bloom *et al.*, 2005) model was also drawn from, emphasising commitment to the coaching process, building trusting relationships, providing fresh perspectives, capitalising on issues to provide rich learning opportunities and adaptability to meet perceived needs, providing emotional support with a focus on organisational goals, all within an ethical approach. A degree of confusion and conceptual overlap between mentoring and coaching was recognised by the national CPD team, which set out to clarify their distinctive features (Alcorn and Taylor, 2006). Clarity was not assisted by the vast range and diversity of government-funded coaching initiatives and models 'developed organically' to varying extents across the 32 local authorities as reported within the evaluative commentary (Finnie, 2007, p. 14). Indeed, the terms 'coaching' and 'mentoring' continued to be used interchangeably.

Coaching and mentoring were thought to hold the key for developing leadership capacity in schools and school systems, along with the means of expanding collaborative practice. Practice and experiential learning were perceived as the means to effect change. Whilst recognition (Finnie, 2007, p. 2) was given to a lack of 'rigorous review and systematic evaluation of coaching and mentoring programmes in education', there was political endorsement for both coaching and headteacher coaches, paving the way for a more formal role for both in government-endorsed headteacher preparation programmes.

Background to the introduction of alternative routes to headship preparation

The publication of *Ambitious, Excellent Schools: Our Agenda for Action* by SEED in 2004 reaffirmed the acknowledgement that headteachers play a vital role in achieving the Scottish Executive's aim to have a modern, world-class education system. It was announced that, from August 2005, all initially appointed headteachers would be expected to meet the SfH (SEED, 2006, foreword). The Scottish Executive (SEED, 2004, p. 13) made a commitment to 'establish new routes to achieve the Standard for Headship, during 2006, to provide choice and alternatives to the Scottish Qualification for Headship (SQH)'.

The Executive launched a consultation process setting out proposals for more flexible approaches. The question of a purely experiential approach based on coaching was debated and is evident in some of the responses to the consultation including the response by the General

Teaching Council for Scotland (2005, p. 4), who made clear, in no uncertain terms, concerns about an over-reliance on coaching and mentoring in the model proposed, and who argued for 'greater recognition [to] be given to the role of the universities'. In addition to discussion about the role and contribution of the universities, there was also discussion related to the relationship between coaching and the achievement of the SfH which looks to holistic development. From this emerged three pilot programmes which were:

- an experiential approach proposed by the CPD Leadership Group and funded by SEED to test flexible approaches using a coaching model;
- a more flexible SQH programme with greater emphasis placed on coaching, devised and funded by the Western Consortium;
- a more flexible SQH programme with greater emphasis placed on coaching, proposed by the National SQH consortia arguing that use should be made of existing structures, funded by SEED.

What follows is brief background to each of those pilots, which leads into discussion of the ways in which coaching and mentoring were utilised, and the impact on the pilot participants.

Coaching and headship preparation programmes

The three approaches grew from a need to widen the pool of potential headteachers, The Scottish Qualification for Headship was designed to enable aspiring headteachers to demonstrate their achievement of the Standard for Headship (SEED, 2005a). These three pilot programmes were the National FRH, The Western SQH Consortium Flexible Route (WC SQH FR) and DARE 1 and 2. The National FRH was developed by the National CPD team and funded by SEED, the WC SQHFR was developed and funded by the Western SQH Consortium, and DARE 1 & 2 were developed by Edinburgh University and funded by SEED. There was one key difference: whereas the National FRH was designed for participants to achieve the professional standard – the SfH (SEED, 2005a) – the other two routes led also to the SQH. Another key difference lay in the selection of participants, whereas the National FRH programme and DARE 1 and 2 recruited experienced school managers, the WC SQH FR decided to test another form of flexibility by recruiting managers of various lengths of experience.

There are, therefore, some key similarities between these different headship preparation programmes. Each of the programmes was a response to the SEED's desire to create more flexibility in pathways to achievement of the Standard for Headship. However, significant differences exist, particularly around the construction of coaching. The key elements of each programme are mapped out in Table 4.1.

Table 4.1: Coaching and mentoring in headship preparation.

Programme	National FRH	Western Consortium	DARE Programme
Programme	An experiential approach to achieving the SfH based on coaching	A more flexible SQH programme with greater emphasis placed on coaching	A Higher Education Institution flexible route with coaching and tutoring elements in SQH programme
Design principles	To demonstrate achievement of the Standard for Headship	To demonstrate achievement of the professional qualification, the SQH	To demonstrate achievement of the professional qualification, the SQH
Roles	Coached programme – full-time coach working with 10 participants	Coaching sessions with trained coach (1:2) and tutoring and assessment with university tutor; school-based mentor	Coaching and tutoring – roles divided in phase 2: a trained coach and tutoring and assessment with university tutor

It is clear that the three pilot programmes – the National FRH, The Western Consortium Flexible Route and DARE 1 and 2 – drew heavily on the extant SQH in the construction of the programme, for example:

- taught elements: residential and day courses;
- group networks;
- use of 360-degree evaluation;
- use of portfolio-based assessment including the development of a portfolio of evidence against the Standard for Headship with an accompanying reflective commentary;
- final oral examination to a panel of professionals.

Where some of the differences lay, was in the extent of school-based work (see Table 4.2). In the Western Consortium SQH FR and more broadly in the DARE 1 & 2, participants had to analyse the school's capability for change, then plan, implement and evaluate a whole-school strategic change programme which then formed the basis of the portfolio and commentary. The school improvement project was summatively assessed

Table 4.2: Learning programme and assessment.

Elements of programme	• residential courses on programme and assessment • 360-degree evaluation • coaching • network meetings • school-based work, if appropriate	• taught programme: the critical self-evaluation and personal learning plan (PLP) • 360-degree evaluation • situational analysis • school improvement project • coaching • tutoring • group reviews	• taught programme: the critical self-evaluation and PLP (Course 1); leading school improvement (SQH double Course 5) • 360-degree evaluation • school improvement project /focus • coaching • tutoring • networks
Assessment	• portfolio and reflective commentary • field formative assessor • oral presentation and viva	• critical self-evaluation and PLP • school improvement project • portfolio and reflective commentary • field summative assessment • viva	• critical self-evaluation and PLP • school improvement project /focus • portfolio and reflective commentary • field summative assessment • oral presentation and viva

through a field visit and through the portfolio and commentary and the final viva. In contrast, the focus of the National FRH was on the construction of the portfolio and commentary to demonstrate achievement of the SfH (SEED, 2005a), which could include previous practice as well as current school-based developments. The balance between prior learning and current practice differed between individual participants on this programme. The different emphasis on the routes between undertaking a school improvement process and the demonstration of the achievement of the SfH shaped fundamentally the role of coaching.

The National FRH model

The National FRH was envisaged as an experiential approach based on coaching. The programme model evolved through use rather than design. An additional pathway was developed around the idea that 'aspiring head teachers would benefit from more focused support' (SE, 2006a, p. 5) provided by a dedicated coach. However, as the evaluation report noted there was 'scant pedagogical justification for the nominated programme elements … Moreover, there was no statement about the nature of the model of coaching to be adopted in the pilot and why this was the preferred model.' As the National FRH developed, there were a common set of activities completed by all participants with the central concern being the personal transformation of participants (Forde, in print, p. 366) through coaching, the focus being on 'enhancing a sense of self-efficacy, self-awareness and communication skills'. In this regard, coaching was pivotal in supporting participants towards demonstration of competence in relation to the SfH.

In the National FRH experienced headteachers, appointed on a full-time basis, supported a maximum of 10 participants each. A coaching contract with targets was agreed for each six-month phase and subsequently reviewed. The coaching sessions followed the rhythm of the programme, starting with discussion of the PLP, discussion of issues arising in school with the latter stages having a substantial focus on the construction and development of the portfolio and commentary. The role of coach was far from traditional, however, in that it incorporated aspects of coaching, mentoring, tutoring and assessment (Forde *et al.*, forthcoming). This inevitably created tensions in the initial pilot, leading to a distancing of the role of coach in the summative assessment stage of successive cohorts.

Western Consortium model

The pilot SQH flexible route devised and funded by the Western Consortium was conceived to provide a more flexible SQH programme and was designed to meet the postgraduate criteria of the SQH programme. Thus, offering a more flexible pathway would 'allow for more individualised learning programmes' (Western Consortium 2008, p. 1). The programme was designed as:

> a mixture of practitioner and academic input will run throughout the course which will be delivered through a variety of modes including: seminars and workshops, self-study activities, ICT interchanges, networks, mentoring and coaching, and one-to-one tutorials. (Western Consortium 2008, p. 1)

In this pilot, participants undertook some key elements of the SQH programme, particularly self-evaluation and the school situational analysis, as preparation for leading the school improvement plan. In the pilot, the goal of coaching was personal transformation but coupled with professional competence in relation to the SfH. This idea of professional competence was constructed in terms of the participant's leadership of a programme of school improvement. A key element of the coach role was to support the development of the participant's personal learning plan (PLP), involving participants identifying relevant learning opportunities through school-based projects and training. The PLP became both a plan for professional development as well as a means of charting and reviewing progress towards the SfH.

Coaching was one of the central processes, but was balanced with in-school development and tutoring. Coaches were drawn from experienced headteachers who had completed a postgraduate qualification in coaching. Each coach worked with up to two participants to undertake one-to-one coaching on a monthly basis in relation to personal and professional change. A staged programme articulated in a coaching handbook included materials and readings as well as activities to support the coach–coachee interaction. An interpersonal contract was drawn up between the coach and participant, with six-monthly reviews of progress with the tutor made in relation to the participant's PLP. A clear distinction was made between the roles of tutor and coach, each having a discrete responsibility in working with the participant. In addition, a field assessor conducted the school visit and assessed the submission with the tutor.

The DARE model

The DARE model was designed to meet the postgraduate criteria of the SQH programme whilst offering a greater degree of flexibility in achieving the SfH. It was proposed that DARE would meet the need for parity between interpretation and understanding of the SfH, and the requirement to evidence impact of professional development. As such, it followed a set of design principles from the outset, based upon the programme as delivered in the South Eastern Consortium.

The distinctive feature of the DARE model comprised additional tutoring, coaching and mentoring through a structured programme. From the outset, it was envisaged that 'pure coaching' would not meet the needs of the pilot participants. Instead, a carefully crafted blend of additional tutoring, coaching and mentoring conversations was envisaged. The distinctions between coaching and mentoring broadly followed that provided by Hanbury (2009, pp. 4–5): 'mentoring which inclines towards guidance and advice and coaching which focuses on developing capacity within individuals to discover their own solutions in an equal and non-judgemental relationship'. Tutoring related to aspects such as advice on course-related matters and the preparation of assignments. In contrast, coaching provided the 'space' within which each participant was able to explore aspects of professional development and practice, and to discuss matters of personal concern or interest.

In DARE 1, additional tutoring, coaching and mentoring were provided by the university's programme director. The multifaceted role of the tutor coach brought with it inherent complexities. As such, in DARE 2 the roles were separated, with the university's programme director continuing to provide the additional tutoring, and experienced head-teachers providing the coaching and mentoring with between one and two participants each. The intention, successful to a degree, was that each participant's PLP would help to ensure progression and coherence in their professional development.

Coaching and mentoring: key themes emerging from the pilots

The aim of this chapter was to begin with a review of developments leading to this point in time where coaching and mentoring have been positioned as desirable elements of leadership preparation, to explore key themes emerging from understandings about leadership preparation and to highlight significant considerations in relation to experiential approaches and their impact on learners, with a specific focus on coaching and mentoring. It is to the latter that we now turn in relation to the three pilot programmes previously introduced.

The nature of coaching

Although coaching by nature is responsive to the needs of the individual and is flexible in its approach, what has emerged across the three pilots is the importance of having a defined purpose, bringing with it the need for agenda-setting between coach and coachee. The defined purpose can vary, but the coaching conversations within a leadership preparation programme do need to be focused, with all involved in the process mindful of the impact sought on professional practice. The identification of desired outcomes, changes in behaviour and strategies to achieve those outcomes, along with examining progress towards realising those desired outcomes, all become part of the coaching conversation. In each of the pilot programmes, the PLP formed a basis to different extents for coaching conversations. Participants were also able to use the coaching conversations as opportunities to reflect on their practice and to identify challenges or barriers to effective practice that they sought to overcome. Defining the capabilities which coaches are charged with helping participants to develop is a challenge. A national SfH of itself is not sufficient. It is the interpretation of the competences in relation to each individual, their stage of development and professional context which is key to the coaching agenda.

Coaching plus

Overall, coaching was highly regarded by participants in each of the programmes. Key outcomes of that coaching experience were increased confidence in relation to participants' perception of their own abilities and in relation to their professional relationships with others. Coaching potentially represented a powerful medium for supporting aspirant headteachers. However, an alternative route based purely on coaching was found to be insufficient in meeting their needs.

Each of the pilot models drew from the complementary roles of tutor, coach and mentor. While there are conceptual differences between coaching, mentoring and tutoring (as discussed by Forde in Chapter 2), evaluation of the three pilot projects would suggest that what they have in common is a focus on 'fostering change' in the individual participant and on their leadership practice in school. The tutor role was charged with an understanding of the processes of adult learning, maintaining a holistic overview of the programme, its design in respect to supporting leadership development, its constituent parts, participants' progress and the requirements for successful completion including the assessment outcomes. The mentor role required knowledge, understanding and experience of senior leadership and management in school contexts, as well as the challenges faced therein, the ability to know when more directed support was required to assist the participant beyond a stuck obstacle in their practice, as well as an understanding of what the SfH looks like in practice. The coach role required the ability to build a trusting relationship (Hanbury, 2009), to actively listen, to challenge underlying assumptions, to provide feedback in a supportive and challenging manner, to facilitate visualisation of a future state, to enable participants to identify their own solutions and to agree goals and then set and review progress (see Table 4.3).

Table 4.3: Roles in alternative routes.

Activities	National FRH	Western SQH Consortium	DARE 2
Coaching	Coach through coaching sessions	Coach through coaching sessions	Coach through coaching sessions
Tutoring	Coach providing feedback on formative tasks	Tutor review of PLP, progress and preparation of assignments	Course-related matters, progress and preparation of assignments
Assessing	Coach acted as assessor for another Local authority cohort	Trained field assessor	Tutor assessed Portfolio and Commentary / Trained field assessor co-assessed Portfolio
Mentoring	Coach through previous experience as headteacher	In-school mentor – headteacher or senior leader	In-school mentor – headteacher or senior leader
Co-ordinating	Project manager for FRH	Local authority SQH Co-ordinator	Dual coordination by University co-ordinator and LA SQH Co-ordinator
Coach support	Coach for coaches	University accredited coaching training programme	Dual support by University co-ordinator and LA SQH Co-ordinator

There are inherent tensions at play between the three roles requiring acknowledgement, regardless of whether the roles are embodied in one individual or separated out. The potential for conflict of interest when one person fulfils all three roles is increased. So, too, is potential bias in the formal assessment components. On the other hand, different and multiple roles have the potential for fragmentation, loss of a well-informed cohesive developmental approach. However, a multiple role approach does draw from a wider pool of expertise.

The qualities of the coach

In these three case studies, the quantity of coaching provided was not of benefit in itself. Coaching at the right times for the right purpose on the other hand was. The quality of the coach was felt to be key to the quality of the coaching (Davidson *et al.*, 2008; Torrance and Pritchard, 2010). This carries implications for the selection of coaches. Coaching aspirant headteachers towards demonstrating competence in relation to a professional standard or publically articulated set of criteria such as the SfH requires a unique set of skills. Unlike more conventional general-ised coaching models, such as executive coaching (Feldman and Lankau, 2005) where a strength of the role is perceived as the coach's externality to the organisation and its purpose providing dispassionate distancing, coaching for leadership development requires experience of whatever standard or set of criteria to be achieved looks like in practice. It also requires knowledge and understanding of overall programme design and assessment components. Such professional knowledge requirements are in addition to interpersonal ability and coaching skill.

One debatable point is whether coaching should be provided by a headteacher, the tension between facilitative (coaching) and instruc-tional (mentoring) dimensions. On the one hand, being a headteacher (skilled or not) does not in itself assure proficiency as a coach. However, given the complementary nature of the coach and mentor role, being an experienced headteacher was found to be advantageous in each of the pilot programmes. So, too, was training for, and experience of, coaching. Recruitment of suitable coaches becomes more problematic the greater the number of participants and local authorities or employers engaged in the programme. It is a challenging role. So, too, is the management of the programme's coaching provision.

Purposeful reflection

Self-reflection for leadership preparation is insufficient in itself. So, too, is mere replication of familiar practice as with a narrow mentoring approach. The coaching process in each of the pilots challenged par-ticipants critically to reflect on their practice, values and beliefs, and to take ownership over their learning (Robertson, 2009). Critical reflec-tion on and in current practice, to inform change for future practice, is key. Goal-setting towards desired outcomes (Blackman, 2010) provides a focus for interaction between coach and coachee, connecting coaching and leadership (Davidson *et al.*, 2008) to support exploration and self-discovery with skilled feedback. Furthermore, critical reflection needs to be both challenging and informed. In each of the pilot programmes, participants drew from feedback from colleagues on their personal quali-ties and interpersonal skills through some form of 360-degree exercise. The place of scholarly activity to inform reflection on current and future practice cannot be overplayed (Brown and McIntyre, 1993). Without it, there is a danger of not moving beyond a cosy, comfortable and familiar frame of reference.

Readiness for coaching

Both coach and coachee need to come ready to engage in the coaching process. The basis for such readiness is the building of a trusting relationship deemed crucially important at the outset in each of the three pilots. A trusting relationship enables participants to reveal their vulnerabilities and areas for further development (Robertson, 2009). Thereafter, the coachee 'must be willing to change' (Blackman, 2010, p. 428), through a process of critical reflection on practice. And, be willing and able to inform changes in their practice. Everything else is just talk.

Selection of a leadership preparation approach

It is difficult for those embarking on leadership preparation and for those charged with supporting their development to be confident about which approach would be most appropriate to supporting each individual. Even for those participants in senior leadership and management positions, it is difficult to ascertain either the extent and depth of their experience, or their readiness for coaching. A nationally agreed initial programme with the same first steps used to inform which approach to follow thereafter, would better support all those involved in the process. As each of the pilots included an initial residential period or taught days, a 360-degree evaluation and the formulation of a PLP based on critical reflection of practice and experience to date in relation to the SfH, it is conceivable that all participants could complete those initial experiences before committing to a specific programme. In so doing, decisions would be informed rather than based on preconceptions.

Sustainability of choice and parity of esteem

The resourcing of leadership preparation will always be an issue because of the significant costs incurred in high quality, intensive professional learning. Of equal concern is the issue of how people learn best. Flexibility is a key component of personalisation and choice. Maintaining choice and flexibility of provision whilst ensuring rigour and parity of esteem is a significant challenge. Experiential approaches using coaching and mentoring need to have parity of esteem in terms of learning outcomes. This necessitates a blended learning approach which combines personal and intellectual development as the basis for leading institutional development.

The sole concern of participants and employers should be the approach best placed to support an individual's leadership development. The quality of provision and support for any approach is dependent on government, employers, schools and universities taking an active interest in the success of a programme and making a clear commitment to the support required to ensure individuals' professional development. Educational leadership preparation takes a combined effort and no one element is sufficient in itself. Consideration is needed at national level as to the development of a single framework within which a range of approaches could be accommodated, clearly articulated to each other to ensure parity of end points. Such a development would need to ensure adequate funding for all approaches and equity in any subsidy provided. The long-term viability of all programmes, to safeguard choice, is predicated on sustainable funding.

Conclusion

We have come a long way since 1998. We know more now than ever before about effective headteacher preparation programmes and yet such programmes are still an 'act of faith' (Cowie and Crawford, 2007, p. 129). How best to support the professional development of school leaders is still the subject of much debate. As the role of educational leaders becomes increasingly complex and challenging (Woods *et al.*, 2007) continued debate is justified. Ultimately, we need to 'ask ourselves what type of leaders we really "want" to create, and what type of leaders we "are" creating' (Robertson, 2009, p. 46). From that, the purpose of a programme for leadership development needs to be determined. A discussion regarding the balance between an emphasis on personal transformation and on ensuring that participants develop the professional capabilities for leading schools then needs to follow. So, too, does agreement regarding any role that a SfH should play. Lessons learned by academics and practitioners should help inform the design of future programmes.

We also know more now than ever before about effective coaching and mentoring within leadership preparation programmes. We understand that the role is complex and requires a discrete set of skills and abilities. We also understand that coaching and mentoring have to work in a complementary fashion to tutoring support. They comprise discrete yet complementary roles. Experienced academic and practitioner support working to a common purpose can only enhance provision.

We have come to appreciate that leadership development is a complex process with no simple answers (Reeves *et al.*, 2002). Sustainable resourcing of high quality, intensive professional learning is a significant issue, particularly in times of fiscal restraint. So, too, is how best to support individuals' professional development and how best to ensure equity of access to provision. If leadership is central to school improvement then coherent but flexible blended learning approaches to leadership development, with parity of esteem with regard to outcomes, are required.

From the various programmes and pilot projects discussed, it is evident that designing, developing and delivering quality headship preparation programmes is extremely challenging. There is no singular ideal model, a balance needs to be struck. Equally clear is the limited financial support available within a system for such provision and the need for available funding to be utilised to best effect. Uncompromisingly, the nature of the levels of one-to-one support required mean that any model will be expensive in real cost terms. Across Scotland as in other systems, we have the skill and capacity to identify and support aspiring heads. To date, we have not used that capacity to best effect.

Fundamentally, a national review of leadership preparation would seem prudent (Torrance and Pritchard, 2010). The challenge still facing programme designers and partner employers is to develop a continuum of viable and cohesive CPD provision providing choice, flexibility and rigour to meet the needs and aspirations of Scotland's future educational leaders. One thing is clear, there is no simple answer or 'off-the-peg' solution (Bush, 2008, p. 127).

The ascendancy of coaching as a mode of leadership development (Bush *et al.*, 2007; Hanbury, 2009) is as much in evidence north as south of the Scottish Border, bringing with it further consideration of who is best placed to deliver support to candidates. From the pilot programmes discussed in this chapter, we have come to understand that coaching in itself is not sufficient. However, a crafted blend of coaching, mentoring and tutoring within a cohesive programme of professional development can meet the needs of aspiring headteachers.

CHAPTER 5

Professional learning communities

Mike Carroll

What is a professional learning community (PLC)?

A common theme in the previous chapters has been the importance of setting processes such as mentoring, coaching and even tutoring and facilitating in a wider context, using different approaches to build collaboration and learning. In this chapter attention now turns a more focused exploration of collaborative approaches to teacher learning, particularly professional learning communities.

Senge (1990) argues that collaborative learning, rather than individual learning, is important in terms of successful and sustainable organisational development as collaborative structures are more likely to result in deeper organisational learning, both collectively and individually. Realising the potential of collaborative learning through information sharing and knowledge creation at classroom, school and system level is particularly important in the face of rapid, technological change (Chapman *et al.*, 2010, p. 53). Consequently, a belief that the quality of learning and teaching can be enhanced by staff working and learning together has led to increased interest in the notion of professional learning communities (Stoll *et al.*, 2003, p. 2). Riley and Stoll (2005, p. 12) provide a useful working definition to help us understand the meaning of the term 'professional learning community' (PLC) with respect to schools as places that 'appear to take a collaborative, learning-centred, enquiry-orientated, development-focused approach to improving learning and teaching for everyone in the school community, most especially pupils'. However, it is worthwhile to indicate that 'there is no universal definition of a professional learning community' (Stoll and Louis, 2007b, p. 2).

What we do have is a sense that we know what they look like, as there is general agreement that PLCs are places where there is a collaborative engagement focused on supporting and taking forward the learning of all members of the community, particularly the learning of students. It is also generally agreed that within a PLC staff critically interrogate their practice in an ongoing, reflective and growth-promoting way (Mitchell and Sackney, 2000) in order that they can develop and maintain the 'capacity to promote and sustain the learning of professionals in a school with the collective purpose of enhancing student learning' (Bolam *et al.*, 2007, p. 18).

The core idea underpinning PLCs of turning our classrooms and schools into dynamic learning communities focused on learning, particularly the learning of students, is highly admirable, but unfortunately will remain little more than rhetoric if this is conceived of as a simple realignment in our thinking or minor readjustment in the way that we organise how we do things in classrooms and schools. Rather, PLCs describe a new landscape of 'connection, relationships, reciprocity, and mutuality' (Mitchell and Sackney, 2007, p. 31), a landscape in which 'teachers are learners who are taught important and interesting lessons by their students, by the broader community, by each other, and by the parents of their students' (Mitchell and Sackney, 2007, p. 31). Consequently, PLCs represent 'a fundamental paradigm shift in the relationships in the organisation' (Martin, 2011, p. 147).

Part of the problem in arriving at a 'universal definition' is that the words contained within the term PLC – 'professional', 'learning' and 'community' – can and do mean slightly different things to different people, at different times and in different places. The aspiration is that they will act in concert to reinforce each other in building more effective relationships and practice (Stoll *et al.*, 2003). The first of these words, 'professional', within the context of a school, would imply that the work of the school is grounded in the distinctive knowledge base of teaching and learning allied to an ethic of care and service orientated towards meeting the needs of different client groups, especially students. However, there is an inherent problem here in that the word 'professional' can be narrowly interpreted as referring to teachers supported by school leaders. Within a classroom context this would immediately exclude a variety of people who support teachers and students (Bolam *et al.*, 2007). Beyond the classroom the notion of 'community' opens out the potential list of people, based inside and outside a school, who can, and frequently do, contribute to the learning of staff and students. Bolam *et al.* (2007, p. 21) indicate that there is an important distinction to be made between those involved in the 'inner core' of the PLC and those who occupy more peripheral positions, and that this 'inside', 'outside' nature of involvement varies between schools and over time. Notwithstanding this caveat, PLCs are seen as being 'inclusive' in that they are open to, and draw upon, the contributions and involvement of all within and beyond the school community, not just teaching staff.

The context of the community is of central importance. However, 'the word community has many meanings but it is used widely because it conveys the sense of individuals working together with shared beliefs and goals' (Riley and Stoll, 2005, p. 2). Within the school context the groups who are working together share a common aspiration of raising achievement and attainment for all students and this extends to all those contributing to this process; consequently the school becomes a community of learners. The notion of the 'school community' within the Scottish educational system is defined in terms of the 'catchment area', which can be crudely delineated by 'a line drawn on a map' to outline a particular neighbourhood area: a geographical community. However, notwithstanding the fact that families from outwith the catchment area of any given school can submit a 'placement request' (that is, request that their child be allowed to transfer across catchment boundaries), the reality is nevertheless more complex as any given geographical community has embedded within it a variety of different communities (for example, different family structures, different faith traditions, ethnicity, social class or political affiliation). This is made all the more complex at an individual level as a result of differing degrees of attachment to the disparate community groupings. Riley and Stoll (2005, p. 5) suggest that 'homogeneous single-class, single-race communities do exist but rarely in large cities'. Consequently, these communities have a kaleidoscopic quality in terms of their composition and level of engagement with the school, as well as being very fluid due to increased population mobility often brought about by fluctuating economic conditions, at home and abroad, as well as political instability.

The challenge facing schools is multifaceted in that they must first map out the disparate communities that form part of the school community; always bearing in mind that they are mapping a fluid landscape.

The second challenge for schools is facilitate a process of bonding and bridging (Putnam and Feldstein, 2003) whereby the disparate communities establish a sense of identity and become more cohesive as a result. The process of bonding, although not unproblematic, is rather more straightforward to achieve as it involves bringing together people who are, in some way, similar. Schools can be very effective at this in bringing together staff. The danger is that if this is all you do, the community that forms will tend to be inward-looking and this will have an impact upon the ability of the community to adapt to change. Bridging, although more difficult to achieve, will in time enhance the effectiveness of the community in which bonding is under way, or has taken place, as this process involves integrating different types of people into the community, which in turn tends to make the community as a whole more outward-looking (West-Burnham, 2009). The ultimate challenge for any school with aspirations to become a PLC is to engage all of the members of the 'community' in professional learning about educational issues in order that they can contribute to the process of school improvement (Huffman and Jacobson, 2003).

The centrality of the final word, 'learning', is significant as it highlights the objective of improvement in learning for all, particularly the learning of students. Learning in the context of professional communities involves working together towards a better understanding of a wide variety of knowledge bases such as the processes of learning, pedagogical concepts and practices and how these are related to learning, educational contexts and the like (see Figure 5.1).

The belief which lies at the heart of the PLC is 'that the quality of learning and teaching can be enhanced by teachers working and learning together' (Stoll *et al.*, 2003, p. 2). Professionals working in education are unlikely to view the proposition that learning is partly a social process (Guile and Young, 2003) as controversial, so it is somewhat surprising that the learning experiences of many members of staff are fragmented, with working in isolation being more the norm (West-Burnham, 2009). This is a concern, as learning involves making connections which, if only accomplished at the level of the individual, means that there is little by way of collective learning and understanding throughout the organisation (Stoll and Bolam, 2005). To frame this differently, no single member of staff can be expected to have a complete grasp of all professional knowledge. Consequently, the learning of an individual is only understandable if we

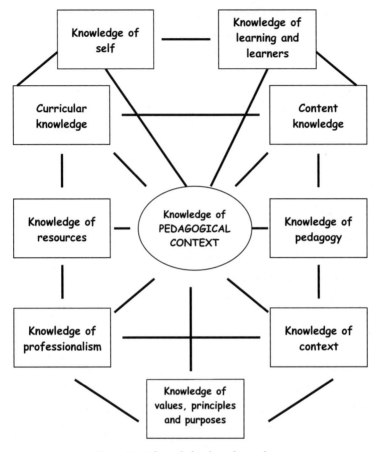

Figure 5.1: A knowledge-based paradigm.

set it within the context of learning within the school system. Essentially, individual learning and collective learning are intertwined, with significant learning processes achieved by collective activities (Carroll, 2009). Hargreaves' (1994) notion of a post-technocratic model of professional development is useful here as it describes a symbiotic relationship between the individual and their school. In the final analysis, learning in a PLC 'is always about people, their lives, and their experiences' (Mitchell and Sackney, 2007, p. 31) set within a way of working in a school designed to encourage collaboration and professional learning with a view to ensuring improvement in the learning of students (Martin, 2011). What, then, are the characteristics of an effective PLC?

Characteristics of a PLC

A study carried out by Bolam *et al*. (2005) determined that effective PLCs exhibited a number of characteristics, and that there was a link between how fully these characteristics are expressed in PLCs and the extent of positive outcomes: the impact on the professional learning and morale of staff, and the impact on students' engagement with learning and their actual learning (Bolam *et al*., 2005). The characteristics of effective learning communities identified included shared values and vision; mutual trust, respect and support; collective responsibility; inclusivity, enquiry-based learning; professional learning; collaboration; and connection.

Shared values and vision

Learning communities have a shared vision, value and goals (Mitchell and Sackney, 2000) and there is a very clear sense of purpose: a culture of improvement in which there is an unwavering focus on the processes of teaching and learning. Within a PLC, learning is seen as 'an iterative process in which learning how to learn is as important as the focus of learning itself' (West-Burnham, 2009, p. 108).

Mutual trust, respect and support

A core value, the 'superglue' that binds PLCs together, is mutual trust (Riley and Stoll, 2005); indeed social trust among members of staff is seen as the strongest facilitator of a professional community (Stoll and Bolam, 2005). Respect is also important as it provides staff with a sense that they have a 'full value contract' with each other by which their efforts and contributions are valued and not 'discounted', providing staff with a sense of self-worth. Effective PLCs are therefore characterised by cultures of trusted colleagues who value each other personally and professionally, and who are committed to the students (Hargreaves, 2007, p. 187).

Collective responsibility

There are high expectations that *all* staff, working collectively, will support and encourage achievement and attainment in every student. Therefore the success of a PLC is a reflection of willingness of its staff to support each other in creating effective teaching and learning opportunities to meet the disparate needs of *all* of the students they serve. Mitchell and Sackney (2007, p. 34) argue that each moment is seen as a teaching moment, and all members of the school community are encouraged to think about what they are teaching and what others might be learning from their actions.

Inclusivity

Membership of the PLC involves all staff, support staff and parents. In addition, the contributions of others are valued as 'the notion of a "community" draws attention to the potential that a broad range of people based inside and outside a school could mutually enhance each other's learning and school development' (Stoll *et al.*, 2003, p. 2). Consequently, staff come to think of the community in holistic terms rather than as one fragmented into several contributing satellite communities.

Enquiry-based learning

Professional learning communities appear to work best when evidence-informed change is incorporated into regular cycles of planning, implementation, enquiry and review focused on learning (Hargreaves, 2007). At the very heart of evidence-informed change lies a process of professional enquiry in which staff are encouraged to engage in a structured reflection on their practice by designing, planning and implementing professional actions with the intention of improving some aspect of their own and others' professional practice for the benefit of others (Dadds and Hart, 2001). Consequently, the process of professional enquiry helps to inform teaching and learning. Time, space and resources are made available to accommodate this. In order to facilitate teaching and learning, staff are naturally involved in knowledge consumption; however, in changing their practice, through a process of challenging assumptions, testing out new approaches and learning together from the results, staff also create new knowledge.

Professional learning

Sammons *et al.*, (2007, p. 214) suggest that you cannot improve student learning without improving the learning of staff, and they argue that staff learn best by sharing ideas and collaborative planning, through the co-construction of learning. Consequently, opportunities for continuing professional learning are identified and promoted, with all staff being encouraged to participate in and value professional learning. In addition, there is a collective drive for staff to support each other with respect to professional learning as the acquisition of knowledge is seen as a social process (Guile and Young, 2003), being a function of interaction between staff as well as something that resides in the individual. The community also recognises that staff who share a desire to learn and improve will be better placed to create stimulating learning experiences for students and for each other.

Collaboration

To create a culture of enquiry staff need to work collaboratively with colleagues and to seek and use external supports from local authorities, universities and other professional groups (Stoll and Bolam, 2005, p. 57). A key concern in collaborative working is to develop positive working relationships, with every member of the community being 'valued as someone with ideas and thoughts to share and with an important role to play' (Mitchell and Sackney, 2007, p. 32). However, although positive relationships are important, the type of interaction evident in collaborative cultures involves staff in opening up their beliefs and practices to critique with a view to improving practice (Katz and Earl, 2010). Central to this is the notion that knowledge lies in different minds, both individual and collective, so the value of collaboration lies in spanning and plugging 'structural holes' where information or skills are lacking (Muijs *et al.*, 2010). In an effective PLC such a process of collaboration extends throughout the community (for example, teachers with support staff) rather than just occurring between specific staff (for example, teachers) with staff working together rather than individually in order to learn from, with and on behalf of others, so facilitating the development of 'socially distributed knowledge, whereby individual knowledge bases become part of the collective discourse and expand the professional capacity of the entire team' (Mitchell and Sackney, 2000, p. 60).

Connection

PLCs forge partnerships beyond the school with other schools, local authority Quality Improvement Officers, other agencies, Colleges of Further Education and universities. This process of developing network-to-network learning enables intelligence gathered on the 'outside' to be processed in order to support the process of enquiry and improvement on the 'inside'. Staff come to value networked learning as they grow in their awareness of how the network can help them challenge and develop their practice through the capacity building and professional learning opportunities afforded to those who participate (Sammons *et al.*, 2007).

Collaborative professional enquiry

Professional learning involves supporting staff in the development of knowledge, skills and capabilities, such that not only does their individual performance improve but that they are better placed to contribute to the achievement of organisational objectives (that is, coaching). This can be directive and involve a more experienced and/or senior colleague inducting a less experienced and/or junior colleague into the ways of practice (that is, mentoring). This professional learning is most effective when it provides learning opportunities for all involved. Robinson and Seba's (2004, p. 6) review of research on continuing professional development (CPD) suggests that

> for CPD to be effective it must provide opportunities to reflect on practice, engage in dialogue, be based in actual work with students and provide opportunities for peer observation, coaching and feedback.

This connection between the learning of staff and that of students is seen as being significant in an Ofsted Report (2004) on CPD where it was argued that there should be a clear focus on the learning of students in CPD as this was more likely to lead to improvements in practice. However, professional learning is a third-order activity in that it is undertaken with the intention of improving teaching which, in turn, seeks to improve the learning of students. There is an inherent problem here as the linkage between staff professional learning and improved outcomes for students is a contentious one, in which an improved understanding of professional practice is taken as a future-orientated 'proxy' measure of improved outcomes for students (Reeves *et al.*, 2003).

Consequently, the model of CPD that involves staff attending a 'course', by itself, no longer inspires confidence in bringing about sustained improvement in outcomes for students. Carroll (2011) suggests that the problem here is that transferring insights of practice, from one location to another, is often unsuccessful as the contextual assumptions for each of the locations involved are different. Consequently, what is required is a form of professional learning that enables insights into practice, no matter their source, to be focused in bringing about solutions to 'practical problems in the lived professional lives of practitioners' (Groundwater-Smith, 2007, p. 60). Professional learning communities offer the possibility of a more sustained form of professional learning, taking place over extended periods, set within the context of professional practice. This more continuous form of professional learning is likely to feature:

- a focus on professional practice and reflection;
- the utilisation of different knowledge bases;
- collaborative activity; and
- dialogic interaction. (Pedder *et al.*, 2005)

One way of realising this is described by Carroll (2009), who outlines a form of personal and professional learning that involves staff working collaboratively with their colleagues on professional enquiries: Collaborative Professional Enquiry (CPE). These CPEs seek to facilitate an informed and structured reflection on professional action with the intention of improving aspects of professional practice. Dialogue between staff is critically important in order to share and understand other people's ideas, thoughts, feelings and aspirations related to teaching and learning. This sharing contributes to collective knowledge and paves the way for the promotion and advancement of new professional knowledge. The creation of a 'discourse community' enables staff to explore the social construction that is their organisational space. It is through coming to understand the mosaic of organisational realities, and the values, beliefs and attitudes that underpin these realities, that the individual perceptions of staff can coalesce, creating shared norms and meanings. The hope is that such awareness will enable staff to navigate the organisational landscape in order to achieve a 'fit' between the new ways of working being promoted and the organisational context (Carroll, 2009) – 'the way we do things around here'. The Vygotskian concept of the 'zone of proximal development' (ZPD) provides an insight as to how, through social interaction and dialogue, the cognitive capability of individual staff is enhanced by engaging in group, problem-solving activity (Vygotsky, 1978). Activity that is challenging at an individual level may be manageable through support (that is, scaffolding) from 'more knowledgeable others' (MKOs) within the group. Therefore a 'collegial' dimension to professional learning enables staff to share and merge their different perspectives with the knowledge that is created being disseminated throughout their professional context.

In mapping the process of CPE (Coleman and Lumby, 1999; Jackson and Street, 2005) it is clear that there are several broad stages or structural elements evident, in terms of the actions undertaken. There is no template with respect to carrying out a CPE (Woolhouse, 2005);

consequently these stages are not always present all of the time. The stages identified include:

Scoping professional environment and progressive focusing in order to identify a work-based 'problem' set within school improvement plan:
- reviewing literature;
- preliminary discussions/negotiations leading to identifying collaborative colleagues;
- preliminary discussions/negotiations leading to identifying the 'problem'.

Taking account of context:
- using local knowledge to probe the identified 'problem';
- tracing connections between the 'problem' and the planning context.

Modification/renegotiation of initial statement of the 'problem':
- clarifying the nature and scope of the 'problem';
- gathering baseline data.

Securing permissions to act:
- securing internal permissions;
- securing external permissions.

Developing a plan for action:
- selection of methods/procedures;
- selection of evaluation procedures;
- defining roles, responsibilities and levels of participation in the implementation of the plan;
- making connections with external networks.

Implementing the plan:
- re-negotiating roles, responsibilities and levels of participation in the implementation of the plan;
- collecting and analysing the data.

Critically reviewing the outcomes of action:
- writing up the findings;
- identifying further cycles.

Disseminating the findings

CPE takes professional learning a stage further as the process of CPE involves staff using educational literature and research evidence, critically reflecting upon their personal and professional values, past experiences

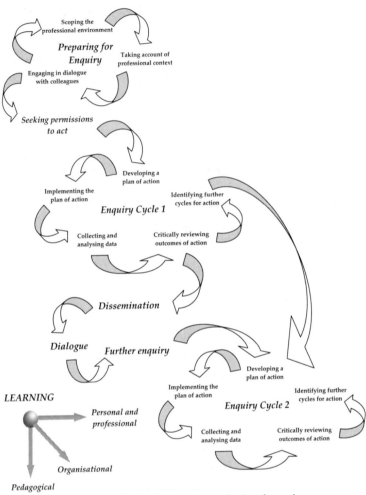

Figure 5.2: Cycle of collaborative professional enquiry.

and educational practice, and on the views of colleagues and students with the intention of bringing about improvement in some aspect of professional practice. This is a form of professional learning which Torrance and Pryor (2001, p. 81) describe as involving staff in progressively developing 'more consciously theorised practice' by 'looping back and forth' between theory and practice, with each informing the other. Through the process of CPE, staff are encouraged to engage in a structured reflection on professional action that is designed, planned and implemented by the staff themselves, with the intention of improving some aspect of their own and others' professional practice for the benefit of others (Dadds and Hart, 2001).

To realise this transformation, staff construct improvement-focused interventions that are:

- persuasive, in that they seek to persuade others and encourage collaborative engagement;
- purposeful and focused, as they aim to change some aspect of professional practice;
- positional, in that they are from the practitioners' perspective; and
- political, in that they aim to change practice and policy in the school. (adapted from Clough and Nutbrown, 2002)

The collaborative dimension to such professional learning enables staff to share and merge their different perspectives through dialogic interaction, so facilitating the development of horizontal expertise, such that they construct knowledge by 'conjoining their understandings in face-to-face interactions with one another over time' (Cochrane-Smith and Lytle, 1999, p. 280). Social interaction provides the context for learning to take place, with staff working and learning together with the intention of developing their practice. Consequently, the learning of an individual member of staff is only understandable if we set it within, and beyond, the context of their PLC, as such individual learning and collective learning become intertwined through the discussions which take place within, and beyond, PLCs.

Networked Learning Communities (NLCs): connections beyond the school

The Networked Learning Communities Programme was a large-scale initiative funded by the National College for School Leadership and the Department for Education and Skills. 'At its peak in 2004 there were 137 school networks involved, including approximately 1500 schools, 25,000 staff and 500,000 pupils' (Hadfield, 2007, p. 262). The 'effectiveness' of this initiative was determined in terms of a number of key outcomes: impact on the professional learning and morale of staff, and the impact on young people's engagement with learning and their actual learning (Bolam et al., 2005). The Networked Learning Communities initiative sought to support schools in working together to enhance professional learning and positive learning outcomes for students (Earl and Katz, 2007). Schools did work together in the past, but this tended to be on an ad hoc basis, largely as a result of the 'professional generosity' of individual staff (West-Burnham, 2009, p. 101). School-to-school collaborative activity was generally rare, with the norm being that schools worked in relative isolation with little by way of lateral learning. The NLC initiative focused on the positive by recognising that is was nevertheless possible for PLCs to 'cross boundaries, both the fuzzy social differentiation that develop between groups, within the school, and the clearer borders that separate the school's members from those in the community and in other schools' (Stoll and Louis, 2007b, p. 4). The aspiration is clearly that in connecting schools in a systemic way we will be better placed to support each other in 'both raising the bar and closing the gap' with respect to professional learning and the learning of students. Before proceeding much further it is important to state that I am not suggesting that the NLC is in some way a superior form of the PLC; both are important!

Although I would suggest that networking and networks are important in a knowledge society, it is important to state that there is no definitive agreement as to what networks are, or what networking means (Earl and Katz, 2007) or of the relationship between professional learning and networked learning (Jackson and Temperley, 2007). Social network theory is often used to help describe the relationships between schools in terms of nodes and ties. A network is a set of actors connected by a set of ties. Nodes are the individual actors (for example, persons, teams, organisations, concepts) within the networks, and ties are the webs of relationships between the actors. There can be many kinds of ties between the nodes and they can be:

- directed (that is, potentially one-directional, as in giving advice to someone);
- undirected (as in being physically proximate);
- dichotomous (present or absent, as in whether two people are friends or not);
- valued (measured on a scale, as in strength of friendship).
  (Borgatti and Foster, 2003)

Church *et al.* (2002) have developed this basic framework in terms of threads, knots and nets. The threads (ties) represent the relationships, the communication and the trust between the actors. The knots represent what the actors do together, the shared purpose that joins them and the activities they undertake together. The net is the 'structure' constructed through the relationships and the joint activities, a structure that staff create, contribute to and benefit from (Earl and Katz, 2007). Consequently, network theory formulated in this way tends to be structuralist in orientation, being less concerned with the personal and professional attributes of individual actors. This does not mean that what is being described is necessarily a formal structure, although it can be so, as they can take on a more organic form depending upon the nature of the relationship between the actors (that is, what drives them to interact and engage in network activities).

The purpose of NLCs is similar to PLCs in that they are fundamentally about learning, albeit that this learning is more extensive in its scope. Recent research suggests that interdependence between schools has enormous potential for fostering system-wide improvement, particularly in the most challenging contexts (Ainscow and West, 2006). Through collaborative working, NLCs develop a capacity to make sense of existing knowledge transferred across contexts and, more importantly, to generate context-specific 'new' knowledge, thus contributing to capacity building across the network (Chapman and Fullan, 2007). Senge (1990) identifies this capacity building as a key feature of organisational learning of which there are six strands:

- pupil learning (pedagogic focus);
- adult learning (professional learning communities a key aspiration);
- leadership learning (at all levels);
- organisational learning space (new organisational learning);
- school-to-school learning (network learning);
- network-to-network learning (lateral systems learning). (Jackson and Temperley, 2007, p. 47)

In order to realise this focus on learning by 'going beyond their boundaries', schools intentionally seek out and establish connections with other schools and agencies. This exposes institutions to different sets of values and ways of approaching their work (Riley and Stoll, 2005), requiring them to consider the prospect of abandoning

> singular pedagogical prescription and standardised practices in favour of pedagogical diversity that is networked together to develop increased learning, validated by references to collective experience and outside evidence, and organized around a common and shared purpose. (Hargreaves, 2007, p. 190)

The networked learning being described here takes place when staff from different schools come together to share practice, talk about pedagogical questions that interest them or to explore issues that are current in the improvement agenda of the school. Staff may also engage in purposeful and sustained activity in order to resolve issues of mutual interest, leading to the co-construction of new context-specific knowledge. This forms part of an ongoing cyclical process of improvement which leads to individual and collective construction of meaning built upon dialogic interaction. For this to lead to systemic change it is necessary for staff to interact with each other to create new meaning which can then be shared with others. Once new context-specific knowledge has been created and shared, the expectation is that it will change what staff do in their classrooms. The hope is that the resultant changes in practice will have a positive impact upon the learning of students as well as promoting professional learning across the system.

Jackson and Temperley (2007, pp. 48–9) suggest that there are four distinct learning processes within a NLC:

- Learning from one another – groups utilise individual differences and diversity through sharing of knowledge, experience, expertise, practices, and know-how.
- Learning with one another – individuals learn together by co-construct meaning.
- Learning on behalf of – learning between individuals from different schools is shared with colleagues within their school.
- Meta-learning – individuals come to learn about the processes of their own learning.

Connections or threads (Church et al., 2002) form between staff in different schools and/or supportive agencies with a view to engaging in improvement-focused activity (knots). Clearly, the objective is that this activity will lead to learning; however, the activity also provides the network with its internal architecture (Jackson and Temperley, 2007, 50) by providing a flexible structure that is determined by those engaged in the activity with a view to realising the learning objectives. In addition, the learning objectives are more likely to be realised if the 'ties-that-bind' (threads) are strong, along with a sufficiently large number of staff being actively engaged in the network to facilitate idea generation. In addition, previous ties increase the possibilities of alliances taking place (Borgatti and Foster, 2003). Katz and Earl (2010, p. 42) suggest that networks also require the presence of some key people or 'boundary spanners' who connect the work of the school to the ideas that emerge from the network in order to exert an influence within their school. 'Boundary spanners' are more likely to be staff who take a lead in developing their own networks in order to share their understandings and engage in a process of enquiry focused on educational issues. Through such a collaborative engagement, the four learning processes outlined above enable staff to generate new knowledge or contextual-situated pedagogical practice (Stoll and Bolam, 2005). The outcomes of such networked activity will not lead to any significant change in practice unless it is actively translated into individual school contexts by staff acting as 'boundary spanners'.

Leadership for learning

In order to meet the challenges in developing a learning culture it is essential that there is leadership for learning. Senge (1990) described this in terms of a 'learning organisation' in which staff at all levels work collaboratively to develop their capacity to improve. Learning organisations actively augment the capacity of staff to pursue a vision of improvement through teamwork rather than by individual endeavour. In PLCs the focus of improvement is on professional learning and the learning of students. In order for this to be the concern of all staff it becomes necessary for school leaders to create a set of working structures and conditions that bring about a culture in which 'leadership for learning' goes beyond role and position to include activities and practices, so stretching leadership activity over many people in the community.

Martin (2011, p. 149) argues that the current hierarchical arrangement of leadership in schools means that 'the creation of the necessary conditions for a PLC is essentially still in the gift of the head teacher'. However, this is not to say that school leaders are in any way resistant, as there is evidence to indicate that they do take steps to support capacity building activity in their school communities (Earl and Katz, 2007). Stoll and Bolam (2005) also suggest that supporting capacity building activity, in order to facilitate school improvement, is a crucial element of the strategic role of school leaders. Although not straightforward, such capacity building is possible within a single institutional context as it is focused and more controllable (Riley and Stoll, 2005, p. 25).

Part of this capacity building involves school leaders in identifying, encouraging and supporting other staff in their school to take a role in leading improvement-focused initiatives. Interestingly, staff who become involved in leadership activities in this way are often reluctant to describe their roles in terms of 'leadership' (Earl and Katz, 2007). What is more important in this context is that school leaders 'who exhibit characteristics of a collaborative leadership or transformational style have greater opportunities for success in developing a professional learning community' (Huffman and Jacobson, 2003, p. 248). The school culture that such school leaders foster leads to them becoming important 'boundary spanners' in facilitating change within NLCs. Taking forward improvement-focused activity within the PLC and realising the benefits of such activity within a network of other PLCs – being part of a NLC – requires a reformulation of leadership activity to include both formal (school leaders) and informal (teacher leaders) leadership for no other reason than that there are insufficient formal leaders to lead the improvement agenda. What is being described here is an expansion in the number of staff, with and without formal positions of authority, engaged in leadership activity, albeit with school leaders retaining authority for the strategic direction of the school. This leadership activity can be multifaceted, including activities such as leading a curricular development team, being part of a planning group (for example, organising a joint staff development event) or being part of a collaborative group (for example, collaborative enquiry group) (Jackson and Temperley, 2007). When leadership is not defined in terms of role or formal position, but is stretched over many people through their engagement in activity, it is described by Spillane (2006) as typifying 'distributed leadership' whereby many people perform leadership work within and beyond the classroom (Katzenmeyer and Moller, 2001):

> leadership does not take on a new meaning when qualified by the term 'distributed'. It still means the exercise of influence over the beliefs, actions and values of others. What may be different is how that influence is exercised and to what end. (Earl and Katz, 2007, p. 255)

Consequently, within such a cultural context the designations of teacher, learners and leaders can become interchangeable as they all provide sources of influence towards improved educational practice. In particular, the role of leaders is not bounded by the school or network as any given leader's sphere of influence operates within, in-between and across the domains of school and network in imperceptible ways.

CHAPTER 6

Taking continuing teacher education forward

Christine Forde and Jim O'Brien

Introduction

This chapter considers some of the issues related to the adoption of experiential (Kolb, 1984) methodologies, particularly the relationship between individual and organisational development. One of the limitations of mentoring and coaching is that in their classic forms this process is deeply individualised, resting on a dyadic relationship of learner and coach/mentor. However, as the policy discussion in earlier chapters intimated, the drive is not just for individual development but also for collegiate working and organisational change. This chapter will consider the strengths and limitations in the use of mentoring, coaching and learning communities as methodologies in the process of continuing teacher development and learning, particularly in relation to institutional reform and improvement and the processes of knowledge creation. The chapter will conclude by examining the place of professional learning in a context of teacher re-accreditation and the expectations of Masters' level qualifications.

Issues related to experiential approaches to teacher learning

For professional learning for teachers to be successful three overarching and essential components are often identified (Burley and Pomphrey, 2011, pp. 22–5): reflection, dialogue and criticality. In their discussion of these concepts, Burley and Pomphrey agree that reflection has been based on too individualistic a view of learning which needs to now take account of location and approaches focusing on groups and/or teams.

With respect to dialogue, so important for the co-construction of learning, distinctions are drawn between discussion and dialogue where discussion may not result in a collaborative outcome. Claims exist about dialogue being essential for transformative learning, favoured in Kennedy's (2005) discussion of models of professional development. Criticality is a key element but requires an inquiring mindset, which Burley and Pomphrey claim is 'greatly enhanced by collaboration and interaction' (p. 25). However, there are potential difficulties.

One of the fundamental issues related to experiential approaches to teacher learning is the question of conformity. One of the stated goals of an early programme of mentoring in teacher induction used in the USA was 'to transmit the culture of the system to beginning teachers' (Hurling-Austin, cited in Ganser 2006, p. 39), but this is a double-edged sword. On the one hand, beginning teachers can strengthen their professional identity by feeling part of a professional community and this will necessitate them understanding and acting within the expectations of that community. On the other hand, professional growth is not simply about learning to follow pre-set routines. Teaching is a complex process, requiring critical thinking and decision making on the part of the teacher as they identify and meet the learning needs of particular groups of learners. The question then faced by mentors is whether they see themselves supporting the learner (whether a novice teacher or leader) to become a critically reflective autonomous professional or one who conforms to the immediate demands and practices of a particular institution. Conformity becomes more prevalent when there is increased accountability or when it is part of career progression, for example when these programmes lead to qualification or accreditation as a teacher. In some settings there is a strong set of unquestioned beliefs about the nature of teaching and learning, and there may well be a subtle pressure to conform rather than challenge what are sometimes deeply held assumptions. For individual teachers, especially new teachers or aspirant school leaders, it can be very risky to challenge these assumptions and the risk can be greater particularly if those teachers challenging assumptions have less experience or status or there are strong affiliative bonds.

There is, then, a built-in conservative tendency in these approaches that highlights a second area of tension, which is the balance between 'sharing practice' and experimentation and innovation. Ingersoll and Kralik (2004) suggest that this construction does not raise the question of whether the practice is effective or not, and were therefore cautious about seeing mentoring as the sole learning process: 'if mentors simply pass on their own teaching practice regardless of whether they are effective or not programs might tend to stifle innovation or the implementation of new approaches on the part of the beginning teachers' (p. 3). The idea of sharing practice is a key feature of mentoring, peer-supported learning and group-based approaches where there could be the development of 'group think' which suppresses rather than engenders genuine questioning and experimentation. What types of knowledge are being developed in such circumstances? A popular concept associated with professional learning is that of 'situated learning' (Lave and Wenger, 1991) or learning from experience involving both practical and procedural knowledge located and understood within a specific context. A problem might be that a closed system is generated, without the potential benefit of external knowledge derived from research elsewhere for example. Here there is the danger that a set of practices are recycled rather than examined critically. Of course, teaching is a deeply contextualised activity, and so practices or ideas cannot simply be copied from one circumstance to the next, but need to be examined critically and either reconstructed or even rejected and set aside. However, again there is a significant danger of the pressure to conform rather than try out different strategies and develop innovatory approaches.

Another issue particularly associated with coaching, but can engage in other forms, is the balance between personal and intellectual development. The professional learning resulting from coaching emerges as a product of social interaction. Bloom *et al.* (2005) argue that we must move from 'ways of doing' to 'ways of being': that is, the interpersonal skills as well as beliefs which are central if change and development is to be achieved. However, there is a possibility that this can lead to an emphasis on behaviours and emotions, and group learning is replaced by group counselling. Berglas (2002) argues that the focus on superficial and short-term changes of experiential methodologies, particularly coaching, might miss some deep-seated psychological issues. We need, therefore, to be very aware of the line between approaches such as mentoring and coaching and specific therapeutic processes. Though inevitably within the experiential pedagogies there will be an element of emotional support, this is not a primary function of such pedagogies. Ecclestone and Hayes (2008), in their critique of 'therapeutic education', argue that 'the slide from engagement of the intellectual to the emotional is very powerful' (p. 116). While such processes might be seen as powerful personally transformative experiences, Ecclestone and Hayes argue that therapeutic education

> is a powerful instrument of social engineering and control because it encourages people to come to terms with being feeble, vulnerable human subject and then allows the state to coach the appropriate dispositions and attitudes of the emotionally well citizen. (p. 161)

This might seem to be an extreme view, but it does point to the importance of considering carefully the nature of professional learning and practice. While personal attributes and emotional well-being are important in teaching and leadership, these are only a partial element of what it is to be a teacher or leader.

Additional barriers are evident when these approaches are seen as individualised, that is, privatised, forms of professional learning. While there is considerable strength in providing development opportunities that focus on the individual practitioner, wider frames of reference can be lacking. Viewing professional learning as an individualised process misses important opportunities for wider benefit (Durrant and Holden, 2005). With a focus on individual development, what happens to organisational improvement? At times like these, with major curricular reform under way, if the focus remains too narrowly focused on individual learning there is a possibility of major disjunction within a school and, at the very least, a blunting of the effectiveness of changes in teaching approach being promulgated.

Thus Robertson (2008), discussing coaching as a leadership development strategy, sees the possibilities of this being a reciprocal relationship; coaching is:

> a learning relationship where participants are open to new learning, engage together as professionals equally committed to facilitating each other's leadership learning development and wellbeing (both cognitive and affective), and gain a greater understanding of professionalism and the work of professionals. (p. 4)

For Robertson, though, coaching is not a stand-alone approach. In these programmes coaching is combined with activities such as action research, working in seminars with academic tutors. In many of the approaches examined in this book the processes of mentoring, coaching, peer-supported or group activities are part of a wider programme of development which draws from experience and expertise in the profession and from research. Thus mentoring is one element in a wider set of activities such as the SQH or the teacher induction scheme. Similarly, in the development of teacher learning communities there is a clear focus on gathering evidence in the classroom and from wider sources to explore and enhance practice.

Being a teacher or a leader is as much an intellectual endeavour as it is an interpersonal process. We need, therefore, to make a clear distinction between therapy and professional learning. Further professional learning is not simply about individualised support, but has to include the development of knowledge and understanding, skills and attitudes as well as personal and interpersonal skills; all are essential for teaching and leadership. The place of knowledge is equally vital across group collaborative processes. The core processes in professional learning communities and other group activities are not just the sharing of but the interrogation of experiences and practices, drawing from a variety of sources: theoretical and research material, the experiences and views of pupils and evidence about learning from the classrooms in the school – this is where criticality comes into its own. In this way ideas and practices are analysed, sometimes confirmed and sometimes reformed to meet changing circumstances. Therefore the core of these professional learning processes is not just 'sharing practice', but the examination of practices based on evidence alongside a critical exploration of the underpinning assumptions on which these practices are based.

We need to reinvigorate the concept of professional learning with a sense of the key place that knowledge and understanding have in helping to explore values and purposes and the practices we use to achieve these. Timperley's (2007) work highlights the importance of knowledge and sustained examination of practice in order to bring about genuine change in practice. Conformity and conservative mindsets are endemic in many educational establishments and may be a continuing by-product of our initial teacher education system. People are often reluctant to 'rock the boat', but at the same time are jealous and protective of their perceived autonomy as professionals. There may be a lack of enthusiasm to engage in a thorough examination of practice because of fears of inadequacy or the fear of criticism or negative feedback. Critique, if done sensibly and sensitively, can be a valuable learning tool, but are we confident that teachers have been and are the reflective practitioners much of the literature claims them to be?

How much preparation and training in mentoring and coaching is available to teachers and is this up to the task? Many teachers now have experience of being a mentor (many fewer have coaching experience), for example through the teacher induction scheme. The evidence suggests (Lord *et al.*, p. 62) that the preponderance of teachers report remaining untrained in mentoring or coaching. Certainly, universities have introduced PG modules on issues such as coaching, practitioner inquiry and practitioner action research. Local authorities have supported teacher induction by training mentors, although, interestingly, this came about after the introduction of the new induction scheme in Scotland. Limited government funding has been evident in support of local coaching initiatives, but not all teachers and schools have benefited from the availability of such opportunities. Yet we are left with a general belief in the efficacy of mentoring and coaching with limited evidence of impact and results. Lord *et al.* (2008) in a National Foundation for Educational Research study for the Training Development Agency in England proffer areas for further research, including investigating group and cross-sector approaches which are doubly relevant given the increasing multi-professional partnerships evident working in current children's services; whether the amount or frequency of support or training influences impact and whether it makes any difference who takes on a mentor role including levels of experience; how models and approaches are selected for particular circumstances and outcomes. The Report (Section 4) comments on the effectiveness to date of mentoring and coaching approaches, advising that the characteristics of effective organisations and management of mentoring and coaching would include:

> providing sufficient time, providing training and support for mentors/coaches, establishing quality assurance and monitoring systems, paying attention to the recruitment and allocation of mentors/coaches, having a clear focus and understanding of mentoring/coaching, and organisational culture and strategic planning. (p. 39)

The Report also highlights a number of key challenges evident in the literature reviewed:

- time and workload pressures and the demands of the mentoring or coaching role allied to a reluctance to take on such roles;
- a limited understanding of the role of mentor and coach in the education sector allied to degree of expertise in the necessary skills;
- reluctance or lack of commitment to engage wholeheartedly with conviction in the process;
- ensuring positive support and challenge and evolving the relationship over time;
- lack of experience and appropriate and sufficient training;
- the possibility of a culture of isolation for teachers influenced by relationships, hierarchies, the ethos, staff morale and team dynamics within schools.

The current economic climate and the cuts or efficiencies expected throughout the public sector indicate that teacher professional development will be at serious risk for the foreseeable future. It is always an identifiable area in which to reduce funding, especially as the 'ring-fencing' of monies allocated for CPD was abandoned some years ago. It becomes perhaps even more critical therefore that schools and teachers are not fully equipped either to engage in collaborative approaches to inquire and research their own practice or to evaluate the impact of what they do on the students they teach.

Teacher education, as now constructed in Scotland, in the wake of the recent review of teacher education *Teaching Scotland's Future* (Donaldson, 2010), is a continuum running from initial teacher education, through induction into career-long teacher learning. In this Report there is clearly an endorsement of the model of teacher professionalism which includes inquiry-based practice, collaboration and career-long development. Further, the Report indicates the possibilities offered by knowledge exchange between school and universities which to date have not been exploited. However, perhaps one of the most significant areas examined in this Report is the question of teachers' career-long development. Tensions around the current system of professional review and development were raised, particularly that this process was not used systematically across the profession. Influences from international examples are clearly evident where in international comparisons one of the key features of the high-performing Scandinavian countries, particularly Finland, is the Masters' level entry qualification. Thus, one of the proposals is for the opening up of 'Masters' accounts' for new entrants to the profession. However, alongside this is the proposal for a Standard for Active Registration:

> a new 'Standard for active registration' should be developed to clarify expectations of how fully registered teachers are expected to continue to develop their skills and competences. This standard should be challenging and aspirational, fully embracing enhanced professionalism for teachers in Scotland. (p. 69)

The Donaldson Report provides an opportunity for all – government, local authorities, schools, teacher education – to reconsider our roles in teacher education and develop a more strategic approach to develop genuine career-long teacher education. However, such a standard is not simply about defining actions, values, knowledge and personal attributes, important as these are. Equally important is the construction of professional learning underpinning an approach to career-long teacher education. We have in the recent past tended to pitch one approach to professional learning against another in seeking the most effective approach. We have to realise that no single pedagogy is sufficient in the process of career teaching learning and, instead, look to programmes and other developmental opportunities which adopt a 'mixed economy' by blending together a range of learning opportunities into coherent, relevant, meaningful and rewarding programmes (Forde and Reeves, 2011, p. 6). From the discussions in this book we can identify that different approaches offer different possibilities but there are some essential features we can map out for this 'mixed economy' (Figure 6.1).

Figure 6.1: Dynamics of a model of learning.

Centre stage has to be a focus on the learning and development of the individual teacher and within this the fostering of a sense of agency in shaping his or her development and practice. From our discussions of different programmes and models, and from our collective experience of designing and delivering programme of continuing development, we can identify three key aspects of professional practice that support the continuing development of teachers:

- the process of reflection;
- the process of enquiry;
- the process of critique.

It is through these three processes that the three essential features of a professional learning process can be brought together: professional practice, dialogue and support between professionals and ideas – whether these are in the form of theory, policy, research or the experience of others. These three processes have to be seen as interactive and mutually dependent to overcome the tensions created by proposing one form of professional learning over another.

REFERENCES

Achinstein, B. (2006) 'New teacher and mentor political literacy: reading, navigating and transforming induction contexts', *Teachers and Teaching*, Vol. 12, No. 2, pp. 123–38

Ainscow, M. and West, M. (2006) *Improving Urban Schools*, Maidenhead: Open University Press

Alcorn, M. and Taylor, F. (2006) *Coaching and Mentoring: Starter Paper*, Edinburgh: National CPD Team

American Confederation of Teachers (AFT) (2001) *Beginning Teacher Induction: The Essential Bridge*, Educational issues Policy Brief 13 (online). Available from: www.aft.org/pdfs/teachers/pb_teacherinduction0901.pdf (accessed 25 February 2011)

Argyris, C. (1976) *Increasing Leadership Effectiveness*, New York: Wiley

Argyris, C. and Schön, D. (1996) *Organizational Learning 11*, Reading, MA: Addison Wesley

Arnott, M. A. (2011) '"The more things change…?" The Thatcher years and educational reform in Scotland', *Journal of Educational Administration and History*, Vol. 43, No. 2, pp. 181–202

Arnott, M. A. and Ozga, J. (2010) 'Education and nationalism: the discourse of education policy in Scotland', *Discourse: Studies in the Cultural Politics of Education*, Vol. 31, No. 3, pp. 335–50

Asia-Pacific Economic Cooperation Ministerial Group (APEC) (1997) *From Students of Teaching to Teachers of Students: Teacher Induction around the Pacific Rim* (online). Available from: www.ed.gov/pubs/APEC/index.html (accessed 3 March 2011)

Berglas, S. (2002) 'Dangers of executive coaching', *Harvard Business Review*, Vol. 80, No. 6, pp. 87–92

Black, D. R., Ericson, J. D., Harvey, T. J., Hayden, M. C. and Thompson, J. J. (1994) 'The development of a flexible, modular MEd', *International Journal of Educational Management*, Vol. 8, No. 1, pp. 35–9

Blackman, A. (2010) 'Coaching as a leadership development for teachers', *Professional Development in Education*, Vol. 36, No. 3, pp. 421–41

Bleach, K. (2001) *The Induction and Mentoring of Newly Qualified Teachers: A Deal for New Teachers*, London: David Fulton

Bloom, G., Castagna, C., Moore, E. and Warren, B. (2005) *Blended Coaching: Skills and Strategies to Support Principal Development*, Thousand Oaks, CA: Corwin Press

Bolam, R. and McMahon, A. (2004) 'Literature, definitions and models: towards a conceptual map', in Day, C. and J. Sachs, J. (eds) (2004) *International Handbook on the Continuing Professional Development of Teachers*, Maidenhead: Open University Press, pp. 33–63

Bolam, R., McMahon, A., Stoll, L., Thomas, S. and Wallace, M. with Greenwood, A., Hawkey, K., Ingram, M., Atkinson, A. and Smith, M. (2005) *Creating and Sustaining Effective Professional Learning Communities (Research Report RR637)*, Annesley, Nottingham: DfES Publications

Bolam, R., Stoll, L. and Greenwood, A. (2007) 'The involvement of support staff in professional learning communities', in Stoll and Louis (eds) (2007), pp. 17–29

Bolam, R. and Weindling, D. (2006) *Synthesis of Research and Evaluation Projects Concerned with Capacity-Building through Teachers' Professional Development*, London: General Teaching Council for England

Borgatti, S. P. and Foster, P. C. (2003) 'The network paradigm in organizational research: a review and typology', *Journal of Management*, Vol. 29, No. 6, pp. 991–1013

Brighouse, T. (2008) 'Putting professional development centre stage', *Oxford Review of Education*, Vol. 34, No. 3, pp. 313–23

Brookfield, S. D. (1995) *Becoming a Critically Reflective Teacher*, San Francisco: Jossey-Bass

Brown, S. and McIntyre, D. (1993) *Making Sense of Teaching*, Maidenhead: Open University Press

Brundrett, M. (2010) 'Developing your leadership team', in Davies, B. and Brundrett, M. (2010) *Developing Successful Leadership*, New York: Springer, pp. 99–114

Brundrett, M. and Crawford, M. (eds) (2008) *Developing School Leaders: An International Perspective*, London: Routledge

Bryce, T. and Humes, W. (eds) (2008) *Scottish Education: Beyond Devolution*, third edn, Edinburgh: Edinburgh University Press

Bubb, S. (2007) *Successful Induction for New Teachers: A Guide for NQTs, Induction Tutors, Coordinators and Mentors*, London: Paul Chapman

Burley S., and Pomphrey, C. (2011) *Mentoring and Coaching in Schools: Professional Learning through Collaborative Inquiry*, London: Routledge

Bush, T. (2008) *Leadership and Management Development in Education*, London: Sage

Bush, T., Glover, D. and Harris, A. (2007) *Review of School Leadership Development*, Nottingham: National College for School Leadership

Calderhead, J. and Gates, P. (1993) (eds) *Conceptualizing Reflection in Teacher Development*, London: Falmer Press

Callaghan, J. (1976) 'Towards a national debate', reprinted in *Education*, 22 October, 332–3

Carroll, M. (2009) 'Chartered Teachers and the process of professional enquiry: the experience of five Scottish teachers', *Professional Development in Education*, Vol. 35, No. 1, pp. 23–42

Carroll, M. (2011) 'Collaborative professional enquiry', in McMahon, M., Forde, C. and Martin, M. (eds) (2011) *Contemporary Issues in Learning and Teaching*, London: Sage, pp. 78–89

Chapman, C. and Fullan, M. (2007) 'Collaboration and partnership for equitable improvement: towards a networked learning system?', *School Leadership and Management*, Vol. 27, No. 3, pp. 207–11

Chapman, C., Lindsay, G., Muijs, D., Harris, A., Arweck, E. and Goodall, J. (2010) 'Governance, leadership, and management in federations of schools', *School Effectiveness and School Improvement*, Vol. 21, No. 1, pp. 53–74

Chi, M. T. H., Siler, S. A., Jeong, H., Yamauchi, T. and Hausmann, R. G. (2001) 'Learning from human tutoring', *Cognitive Science*, Vol. 25, No. 4, pp. 471–533

Christie, D. (2003) 'Competences, benchmarks and standards in teaching', in Bryce, T. and Humes, W. (eds) (2003) *Scottish Education, Post Devolution*, second edn, Edinburgh: Edinburgh University Press, pp. 952–63

Christie, F. and O'Brien, J. (2005) 'A CPD framework for Scottish teachers: steps or stages, continuity or connections?', in Alexandrou, A., Field, K. and Mitchell, H. (eds) (2005) *The Continuing Professional Development of Educators: Emerging European Issues*, London: Symposium, pp. 93–110

Church, M., Bitel, M., Armstrong, K., Fernando, P., Gould, H., Joss, S., Marwaha-Diedrich,

M., de la Torre, A. L. and Vouhé, C. (2002) *Participation, Relationships and Dynamic Change: New Thinking on Evaluating the Work of International Networks (Working Paper No. 121)*, London: University College London

Clough, P. and Nutbrown, C. (2002) *A Student's Guide to Methodology*, London: Sage

Cochrane-Smith, M. and Lytle, S. (1999) 'Relationships of knowledge and practice: teacher learning in communities', in Iran-Nejad, A. and Pearson, P. D. (eds) *Review of Research in Education, Vol. 24*, Washington, DC: American Education Research Association, pp. 249–306

Coleman, M. and Lumby, J. (1999) 'The significance of site-based practitioner research in educational management', in Middlewood, D., Coleman, M. and Lumby, J. (eds) (1999) *Practitioner Research in Education: Making a Difference*, London: Paul Chapman, pp. 1–19

Conlon, T. (2004) 'A failure of delivery: the United Kingdom's New Opportunities Fund programme of teacher training in information and communications technology', *Journal of In-Service Education*, Vol. 30, No. 1, pp. 115–39

Construction Industry Council (1986) *CPD Information Sheets for the Professional Institution Members of the CPD in Construction Group*, London: CIC

Costa, A. L. and Kallick, B. (1993) 'Through the lens of a critical friend', *Educational Leadership*, Vol. 51, No. 2, pp. 49–51

Cowie, M. (2005) 'A silver lining with a grey cloud? The perspective of unsuccessful participants in the Scottish Qualification for Headship programme across the north of Scotland', *Journal of In-Service Education*, Vol. 31, No. 2, pp. 393–410

Cowie, M. (2008) 'The changing landscape of head teacher preparation in Scotland' in Brundrett, M. and Crawford, M. (eds) (2008) *Developing School Leaders: An International Perspective*, London: Routledge, pp. 23–40

Cowie, M. and Crawford, M. (2007) 'Principal preparation: still an act of faith?', *School Leadership and Management*, Vol. 27, No. 2, pp. 129–46

Cullingford, C. (2006) (ed.) *Mentoring in Education: An International Perspective*, Aldershot: Ashgate

CUREE for DfES (2005) *National Framework for Mentoring and Coaching*, report for DfES, London: DfES

Dadds, M. (1997) 'Continuing professional development: nurturing the expert within', *British Journal of In-Service Education*, Vol. 23, No. 1, pp. 31–8

Dadds, M. and Hart, S. (2001) *Doing Practitioner Research Differently*, London: RoutledgeFalmer

Dahlgren, L. O., Eriksson, B. E., Gyllenhammar, H., Korkeila, M., Saaf-Rothoff, A., Wernson, A. and Seeberger, A. (2006) 'To be and to have a critical friend in medical teaching', *Medical Education*, Vol. 40, No. 1, pp. 72–8.

Daresh, J. (2004) 'Mentoring school leaders: professional promise or predictable problems?', *Educational Administrative Quarterly*, Vol. 40, No. 4, pp. 495–517

Darling-Hammond, L. Chung Wei, R., Andree, A., Richardson, N. and Orphanos, S. (2009) *Professional Learning in the Learning Profession: A Status Report on Teacher Development in the United States and Abroad*, Stanford, CA: National Staff Development Council and The School Redesign Network at Stanford University

Daugherty, R. (ed.) (2006) Themed issue on education policy in Wales in the era of political devolution, *Welsh Journal of Education*, Vol. 14, Nos. 1 and 2

Davidson, J., Forde, C., Gronn, P., MacBeath, P., Martin, M. and McMahon, M. (2008) *Towards a "Mixed Economy" of Head Teacher Development: Evaluation Report to the Scottish Government on the Flexible Routes to Headship Pilot*, report by the Universities of

Cambridge and Glasgow: Edinburgh: Scottish Government

Davies, B. and Ellison, L. (1994) 'New perspectives on developing school leaders', *British Journal of In-Service Education*, Vol. 20, No. 3, pp. 361–71

Day, C. (1999) *Developing Teachers: The Challenges of Lifelong Learning*, London: Falmer Press

Day, C. (2002) 'School reform and transitions in teacher professionalism and identity', *International Journal of Educational Research*, Vol. 37, No. 8, pp. 677–92

Day, C. (2005) 'The UK policy for school leadership: uneasy transitions', in Bascia, N., Cumming, A. Datnow, A., Leithwood, K. and Livingstone, D. (eds) (2005) *International Handbook of Educational Policy*, Dordrecht: Springer, pp. 393–420

Day, C. and Gu, Q. (2007) 'Variations in the conditions for teachers' professional learning and development: sustaining commitment and effectiveness over a career', *Oxford Review of Education* [Special issue], Vol. 33, No. 4, pp. 423–43

DES (1972) *Teacher Education and Training* (James Report), London: HMSO

DfEE (1998) *Teachers: Meeting the Challenge of Change*, London: DfEE

DfEE (2001) *Learning and Teaching: A Strategy for Professional Development* (the Green Paper) London: HMSO

Devos, A. (2010) 'New teachers, mentoring and the discursive formation of professional identity', *Teaching and Teacher Education*, Vol. 26, No. 5, pp. 1219–23

Donaldson, G. (2010) *Teaching Scotland's Future: Report of a Review of Teacher Education in Scotland*, Edinburgh: Scottish Government

Draper, J., Christie, F. and O'Brien, J. (2005) 'Meeting the standard? The new teacher induction scheme in Scotland', in Townsend, T. and Bates, R. (eds) (2005) *Handbook of Teacher Education: Globalization, Standards and Professionalism: Teacher Education in Times of Change*, Dordecht: Springer-Kluwer, pp. 391–406

Draper, J. and O'Brien, J. (2006) *Induction: Fostering Career Development at All Stages*, Edinburgh: Dunedin Academic Press

Driscoll, L. G., Parkes, K. A., Tilley, L., Gresilda, A. and Brill, J. M. (2009) 'Navigating the lonely sea: peer mentoring and collaboration among aspiring women scholars', *Mentoring and Tutoring*, Vol. 17, No. 1, pp. 5–21

DuFour, R. (2004) 'What is a "Professional Learning Community"'?, *Educational Leadership*, May, pp. 1–6

DuFour, R., DuFour, R., Eaker, R. and Many, T. (2006) *Learning by Doing: A Handbook for Professional Learning Communities at Work*, Bloomington: Solution Tree

Durrant, J. and Holden, G. (2005) *Teachers Leading Change: Doing Research for School Improvement*, London: Sage

Earl, L. and Katz, S. (2002) 'Leading schools in a data rich world', in Leithwood, K. and Hallinger, P. (eds) (2002) *Second International Handbook of Educational Leadership and Administration*, Dordrecht: Kluwer Academic, pp. 1003–22

Earl, L. and Katz, S. (2007) 'Leadership in networked learning communities: defining the terrain', *School Leadership and Management*, Vol. 27, No. 3, pp. 239–58

Earley, P.,Weindling, D., Bubb, S. and Glenn, M. (2008) *Evaluation of the Future Leaders Pilot Programme: Final Report (Years 1 and 2)*, Project Report, National College of Leadership of Schools and Children's Services (online). Available from: www.nationalcollege.org.uk/index/docinfo.htm?id=21872 (accessed 12June 2011)

Earley, P, Weindling, D., Bubb, S. and Glenn, M. (2009) 'Future leaders; the way forward?', *School Leadership and Management*, Vol. 29, No. 3, pp. 295–306

Ecclestone, K. and Hayes, D. (2008) *The Dangerous Rise of Therapeutic Education*, London: Routledge

Educational Institute for Scotland (2010) *The EIS and Leadership in Schools*, Edinburgh: EIS

Ehrich, L., Hansford, B. and Tennent, L. (2004) 'Formal mentoring programs in education and other professions: a review of the literature', *Educational Administrative Quarterly*, Vol. 40, No. 4, pp. 518–40

Ehrich, L. C., Tennent, L. and Hansford, B. C. (2002) 'A review of mentoring in education: some lessons for nursing', *Contemporary Nurse*, Vol. 12, No. 3, pp. 253–64

Eraut, M. (1994) *Developing Professional Knowledge and Competence*, London: Falmer Press

Evans, L. (2002) 'What is teacher development?', *Oxford Review of Education*, Vol. 28, No. 1, pp. 123–38

Farrell, T. (2001) 'Critical friendships: colleagues helping each other develop', *ELT Journal*, Vol. 54, No. 4, pp. 368–74

Feiman-Nemser, S. (2001) 'From preparation to practice: designing a continuum to strengthen and sustain teaching', *Teachers' College Record*, Vol. 103, No. 6, pp. 1013–55

Feldman, D. C. and Lankau, M. J. (2005) 'Executive coaching: a review and agenda for future research', *Journal of Management*, Vol. 31, No. 6, pp. 829–48

Finnie, G. (2005) *Coaching and Mentoring Update*, Edinburgh: Scottish Government

Finnie, G. (2007) *Coaching and Mentoring Projects – Commentary*, Edinburgh: Scottish Government

Forde, C. (2011) 'Leadership for learning: educating educational leaders', in T. Townsend and J. Macbeath (eds) (2011) *The International Handbook of Leadership for Learning*, Dordrecht: Springer, pp. 353–72

Forde, C., McMahon, M., Gronn, P. and Martin, M. (forthcoming) 'Being a leadership development coach: a multi-faceted role', *Educational Management, Administration and Leadership*

Forde, C., McMahon, M., McPhee, A. and Patrick, F. (2006) *Professional Development, Reflection and Enquiry*, London: Paul Chapman

Forde, C. and Reeves, J. (2011) *The Learning Programme*, Glasgow: Western SQH Consortium

Fournies, F. F. (2000) *Coaching For Improved Work Performance*, London: McGraw-Hill

Friedman, A., Hurran, N. and Durkin, C. (1999) 'Good Practice in CPD among UK professional associations', *Continuing Professional Development*, Vol. 2, No. 2, pp. 52–68

Friedman, A. and Phillips, M. (2004) 'Continuing professional development: developing a vision', *Journal of Education and Work*, Vol. 17, No. 3, pp. 361–76

Fullan, M. (1991) *The New Meaning of Educational Change*, second edn, London: Cassell

Furlong, J. (2005) 'New Labour and teacher education: the end of an era', *Oxford Review of Education*, Vol. 31, No. 1, pp. 119–34

Furlong, J., Barton, L., Miles, S., Whiting, C. and Whitty, G. (2000) *Teacher Education in Transition: Reforming Professionalism*, Buckingham: Open University Press

Ganser, T. (2006) 'A status report on teacher mentoring programmes in the United States', in Cullingford, C. (ed.) (2006) *Mentoring in Education: An International Perspective*, Aldershot: Ashgate, pp. 33–55

General Teaching Council for Scotland (2005) *Response to Ambitious, Excellent Schools: Leadership Discussion Paper*, Edinburgh: GTCS

General Teaching Council for Scotland (2006a) *The Standard for Teacher Education*, Edinburgh: GTCS

General Teaching Council for Scotland (2006b) *The Standard for Full Registration*, Edinburgh: GTCS

General Teaching Council for Scotland (2009) *The Standard for Chartered Teacher*, Edinburgh: GTCS

General Teaching Council for Scotland (2010) *Professional Standards Committee: Starter Paper on Leadership*, Edinburgh: GTCS

General Teaching Council for Scotland (2011a) *Teacher Researcher Programme* (online). Available from: www.gtcs.org.uk/professional-development/teacher-researcher-programme.aspx (accessed 4 June 2011)

General Teaching Council for Scotland (2011b) *Teacher Induction Scheme* (online). Available from: www.gtcs.org.uk/probation/teacher-induction-scheme.aspx (accessed 25 February 2011)

General Teaching Council for Wales (2002) *CPD: An Entitlement for All*, advice to the Welsh Assembly Government, Cardiff: GTCW

General Teaching Council for Wales (2006) *A Professional Development Framework for Teachers in Wales: Professional Development, Recognition and Accreditation (Strand 2)*, advice to the Welsh Assembly Government, Cardiff: GTCW

Golby, M. and Appleby, R. (1995) ' Reflective practice through critical friendships: some possibilities', *Cambridge Journal of Education*, Vol. 25, No. 2, pp. 149–60

Gronn, P., MacBeath, J., Davidson, J., Forde, C., Martin, M. and McMahon, M. (2008) *Towards a 'Mixed Economy' of Head Teacher Development: Evaluation Report to the Scottish Government*, Edinburgh: Scottish Government (online). Available from: www.scotland.gov.uk/Publications/2008/09/30142043/0 (accessed 11 August 2010)

Groundwater-Smith, S. (2007) 'Questions of quality in practitioner research', in Ponte, P. and Smit, B. H. J. (eds) (2007), *The Quality of Practitioner Research: Reflections on the Position of the Researcher and the Researched*, Rotterdam: Sense Publishers, pp. 57–64

Guile, D. and Young, M. (2003) 'Transfer and transition in vocational education: some theoretical considerations', in Tuomi-Gröhm, T. and Engeström, Y. (eds) (2003) *Between School and Work: New Perspectives on Transfer and Boundary Crossing*, Oxford: Pergamon, pp. 63–84

Gunter, H. M. and Forrester, G. (2009) 'School leadership and education policy-making in England', *Policy Studies*, Vol. 30, No. 5, pp. 495–511

Hadfield, M. (2007) 'Co-leaders and middle leaders: the dynamic between leaders and followers in networks of schools', *School Leadership and Management*, Vol. 27, No. 3, pp. 259–83

Hanbury, M. (2009) *Leadership Coaching: An Evaluation of the Effectiveness of Leadership Coaching as a Strategy to Support Succession Planning*, Nottingham: National College for Leadership of Schools and Children's Services

Hargreaves, A. (2007) 'Sustainable professional learning communities', in Stoll and Louis (eds) (2007a), pp. 181–95

Hargreaves, D. (1994) 'The new professionalism: the synthesis of professional and institutional development', *Teaching and Teacher Education*, Vol. 10, No. 4, pp. 423–8

Harland, J. and Kinder, K. (1997) 'Teachers' continuing professional development: framing a model of outcomes', *Journal of In-Service Education*, Vol. 23, No. 1, pp. 71–84

Harris, A. and Jones, M. (2010) 'Professional learning communities and system improvement', *Improving Schools*, Vol. 13, No. 2, pp. 172–81

Hartley, J. and Hinksman, B. (2003) *Leadership Development: A Systematic Review of the Literature. Report for the NHS Leadership Centre*, Warwick: Warwick Institute of Governance and Public Management, Warwick Business School, University of Warwick

Her Majesty's Inspectorate of Education (2006) *Improving Scottish Education: A Report by HMIE on Inspection and Review 2002–2005*, Livingston: HMIe

Her Majesty's Inspectorate of Education (2007) *Leadership for Learning: The Challenges of Leading in a Time of Change*, Livingston: HMIe

Her Majesty's Inspectorate of Education (2010) *Learning Together: Lessons about School*

Improvement – An HMIe Report on How Schools Get Better, Livingston: HMIe

Hewton, E. (1988) *School Focused Staff Development: Guidelines for Policy Makers*, Lewes: Falmer Press

Hobson, A. (2003) *Mentoring and Coaching for New Leaders*, Nottingham, National College for School Leadership

Hobson, A. J., Ashby, P., Maderz, A. and Tomlinson, P. D. (2009) 'Mentoring beginning teachers: what we know and what we don't', *Teaching and Teacher Education*, Vol. 25, No. 1, pp. 207–16

Hord, S. M. (2004) *Learning Together, Leading Together: Changing Schools through Professional Learning Communities*, New York: Teachers' College Press

Huffman J. B. and Hipp, K. K. (2003) *Reculturing Schools as Professional Learning Communities*, Lanham, MD: Scarecrow Education

Huffman, J. and Jacobson, A. (2003) 'Perceptions of professional learning communities', *International Journal of Leadership in Education*, Vol. 6, No. 3, pp. 239–50

Hulme, M., Baumfield, V. and Payne, F. (2009) Building capacity through teacher enquiry: the Scottish schools of ambition, *Journal of Education for Teaching*, Vol. 35, No. 4, pp. 409–24

Hurling-Austin, L. (1990) 'Teacher induction programs and internships', in Houston, W. R., Haberman, M. and Sikula, J. (eds) (1990) *Handbook of Research on Teacher Education*, New York: Macmillan, pp. 535–48

Hustler, D., McNamara, O., Jarvis, J., Londra, M. and Campbell, A. (2003) *Teachers' Perceptions of Continuing Professional Development*, DfES Research Report 429, Nottingham: DfES Publications

Ingersoll, R. and Kralik, J. M. (2004) *The Impact of Mentoring on Teacher Retention: What the Research Says*, Education Commission of the States, Research Review February 2004 (online). Available from: www.ecs.org/html/Document.asp?chouseid=5036 (accessed 17 June 2011)

Ives, Y. (2008) 'What is "coaching"? An exploration of conflicting paradigms', *International Journal of Evidence Based Coaching and Mentoring*, Vol. 6, No. 2, pp. 100–110

Jackson, D. and Street, H. (2005) 'What does "collaborative enquiry" look like?', in Street, H. and Temperley, J. (eds) (2005) *Improving schools through Collaborative Enquiry*, London: Continuum: pp. 41–70

Jackson, D. and Temperley, J. (2007) 'From professional learning community to networked learning community', in Stoll and Louis (eds) (2007a), pp. 45–62

Jackson, P. (2005) 'How do we describe coaching? An exploratory development of a typology of coaching based on the accounts of UK-based practitioners', *International Journal of Evidence Based Coaching and Mentoring*, Vol. 3, No. 2, pp. 45–60

Katz, S. and Earl, L. (2010) 'Learning about networked learning communities', *School Effectiveness and School Improvement*, Vol. 21, No. 1, pp. 27–51

Katzenmayer, M. and Moller, G. (2001) *Awakening the Sleeping Giant: Helping Teachers Develop as Leaders*, Thousand Oaks, CA: Corwin Press

Kelchtermans, G. (2004) 'CPD for professional renewal: moving beyond knowledge for practice', in Day, C. and Sachs, J. (eds) (2004) *International Handbook on the Continuing Professional Development of Teachers*, Maidenhead: Open University Press, pp. 217–37

Kelchtermans, G. and Ballet, K. (2002) 'The micropolitics of teacher induction: a narrative- biographical study on teacher socialisation', *Teaching and Teacher Education*, Vol. 18, No. 1, pp. 105–20

Kennedy, A. (2005) 'Models of continuing professional development (CPD): a framework for analysis', *Journal of In-Service Education*, Vol. 31, No. 2, pp. 235–50

Kennedy, A. (2007) 'Continuing professional development (CPD) policy and the discourse of teacher professionalism in Scotland', *Research Papers in Education*, Vol. 22, No. 1, pp. 95–111

Kennedy, A. (2011) 'Collaborative continuing professional development (CPD) for teachers in Scotland: aspirations, opportunities and barriers', *European Journal of Teacher Education*, Vol. 34, No. 1, pp. 25–41

Kerwood, J. and Clements, S. (1986) 'A strategy for school-based staff development', in Day, C. and Moore, R. (eds) (1986) *Staff Development in the Secondary School: Management Perspectives*. London: Croom Helm, pp. 209–28

Kolb, D. A. (1984) *Experiential Learning: Experience as the Source of Learning and Development*, Englewood Cliffs, NJ: Prentice Hall

Lave, J. and Wenger, E. (1991) *Situated Learning: Legitimate Peripheral Participation*, Cambridge: Cambridge University Press

Le Cornu, R. (2005) 'Peer mentoring: engaging pre-service teachers in mentoring one another', *Mentoring and Tutoring*, Vol. 13, No. 3, pp. 355–66

Little, P. F. B. (2005) 'Peer coaching as a support for collaborative teaching', *Mentoring and Tutoring*, Vol. 13, No. 1, pp. 83–94

Long, J. (2009) 'Assisting beginning teachers and school communities to grow through extended and collaborative mentoring experiences', *Mentoring and Tutoring*, Vol. 17, No. 4, pp. 317–27

Lord, P., Atkinson, M. and Mitchell, H. (2008) *Mentoring and Coaching for Professionals: A Study of the Research Evidence*, Report for the Training and Development Agency for Schools, Slough: National Foundation for Educational Research

Lu, H.-L. (2010) 'Research on peer coaching in pre-service education – a review of literature', *Teaching and Teacher Education*, Vol. 26, No. 4, pp. 748–53

MacBeath, J., Gronn, P., Opfer, D., Lowden, K., Forde, C., Cowie, M. and O'Brien, J. (2009) *The Recruitment and Retention of Headteachers in Scotland: Report to the Scottish Government*, report by the Universities of Cambridge and Edinburgh, Edinburgh: Scottish Government

Mahony, P. and Hextall, I. (2000) *Reconstructing Teaching: Standards, Performance and Accountability*, London: RoutledgeFalmer

Martin, M. (2011) 'Professional learning communities', in McMahon, M., Forde, C. and Martin, M. (eds) (2011) *Contemporary Issues in Learning and Teaching*, London: Sage, pp. 142–52

Martin, M. and Rippon, J. (2003) 'Teacher induction: personal intelligence and the mentoring relationship', *Journal of In-Service Education*, Vol. 29, No. 1, pp. 141–62

McLean, M. (2003) 'What can we learn from facilitator and student perceptions of facilitation skills and roles in the first year of a problem-based learning curriculum?', *BMC Medical Education*, Vol. 3, No. 9 (online). Available from: www.biomedcentral.com/1472–6920/3/9 (accessed 24 January 2011)

McMahon, M., Forde, C. and Martin, M. (eds) (2011) *Contemporary Issues in Learning and Teaching*, London: Sage

Menter, I., Holligan, C., Mthenjwa, V. and Hair, M. (2003) *Insight 8. Scottish Qualification for Headship: Key Issues from the Evaluation*, Edinburgh: Scottish Executive

Mitchell, C. and Sackney, L. (2000) *Profound Improvement: Building Capacity for a Learning Community*, Lisse, Netherlands: Swets and Zeitlinger

Mitchell, C. and Sackney, L. (2007) 'Extending the learning community: a broader perspective embedded in policy', in Stoll and Louis (eds) (2007a), pp. 30–44

Montgomery, A. and Smith, A. (2006) 'Teacher education in Northern Ireland: policy variations since devolution', *Scottish Educational Review*, Vol. 37, pp. 46–58

Moore, T. (2009) 'Enhancing the world of educational quality: peer mentoring processes to retain quality elementary male teachers in Australian contexts', *Curriculum and Teaching*, Vol. 24, No. 2, pp. 59–74

Muijs, D., West, M. and Ainscow, M. (2010) 'Why network? Theoretical perspectives on Networking', *School Effectiveness and School Improvement*, Vol. 21, No. 1, pp. 5–26

National Assembly for Wales (2001) *The Learning Country: A Comprehensive Education and Lifelong Learning Programme to 2010 in Wales*, Cardiff: National Assembly for Wales

National CPD Team (n.d.) *Coaching and Mentoring Summary*, Edinburgh: Learning and Teaching Scotland

Neville, A. J. (1999) 'The problem-based learning tutor: Teacher? Facilitator? Evaluator?', *The Medical Teacher*, Vol. 21, No. 4, pp. 393–401

O'Brien, J. (2007) 'Control or empowerment? The professional learning of Scottish teachers in the post McCrone era', in Pickering, J., Pachler, N. and Daly, C. (eds) (2007) *New Designs for Teachers' Professional Learning*, Bedford Way Papers No. 27, London: Institute of Education, pp. 219–41

O'Brien, J. (2009) 'Teacher induction: does Scotland's approach stand comparison?', *Research in Comparative and International Education*, Vol. 4, No. 1, pp. 42–52

O'Brien, J. and Christie, F. (2005) 'Characteristics of support for beginning teachers: evidence from the new induction scheme in Scotland', *Mentoring and Tutoring*, Vol. 13, No. 2, pp. 189–203

O'Brien, J. and Draper, J. (2001) 'Developing effective school leaders? Initial views of the Scottish Qualification for Headship (SQH)', *Journal of In-Service Education*, Vol. 27, No. 1, pp. 109–21

O'Brien, J. and Hunt, G. (2005) 'A new professionalism? Becoming a chartered teacher – part I', *Teacher Development*, Vol. 9, No. 3, pp. 383–401

O'Brien, J. and Sharp, S. (2008) *Developing Alternative Routes to School Headship: Evaluation of the University DARE Programme, 2007–8*, Edinburgh: University of Edinburgh Centre for Educational Leadership

O'Brien, J. and Torrance, D. (2006) 'Professional learning for school principals: developments in Scotland', *Education Research and Perspectives*, Vol. 32, No. 2, pp. 165–81

Ofsted (Office for Standards in Education) (2004) *Making a Difference: the Impact of Award-Bearing In-Service Training on School Improvement*, London: HMSO

Ofsted (2006) *The Logical Chain: Continuing Professional Development in Effective Schools*, London: HMSO

Organisation for Economic Co-operation and Development (2007) *Quality and Equity of Schooling in Scotland*, Paris: OECD

Opfer, D. and Pedder, D. (2010) 'Benefits, status and effectiveness of continuous professional development for teachers in England', *Curriculum Journal*, Vol. 21, No. 4, pp. 413–31

Opfer, D. and Pedder, D. (2011) 'The lost promise of teacher professional development in England', *European Journal of Teacher Education*, Vol. 34, No. 1, pp. 3–24

Oti, J. (2009) 'Mentoring in FE: staff perceptions', paper presented at the British Educational Research Association Annual Conference, University of Manchester, 2–5 September

Ozga, J. (2005) 'Modernizing the education workforce: a perspective from Scotland', *Educational Review*, Vol. 57, No. 2, pp. 207–19

Pask, R. and Joy, B. (2007) *Mentoring-Coaching: A Handbook for Education Professionals*, Maidenhead: Open University Press / McGraw Hill Education

Paterson, L. (2000) *Education and the Scottish Parliament*, Edinburgh: Dunedin Academic Press

Patrick, F., Forde, C. and McPhee, A. (2003) 'Challenging the "new professionalism": from managerialism to pedagogy?', *Journal of In-Service Education*, Vol. 29, No. 2, pp. 237–54

Pedder, D., James, M. and MacBeath, J. (2005) 'How teachers value and practise professional learning', *Research Papers in Education*, Vol. 20, No. 3, pp. 209–243

Pedder, D., Storey, A. Opfer, V. D. and McCormick, R. (2009) *Schools and Continuing Professional Development (CPD) in England – State of the Nation Research Project (T34718): Synthesis Report*, London: Training and Development Agency for Schools

Phillips, M., Cruickshank, I. and Friedman, A. (2002) *Continuing Professional Development: Evaluation of Good Practice*, Bristol: Professional Associations Research Network

Phillips, R. (2003) 'Education policy, comprehensive schooling and devolution in the disunited Kingdom: an historical "home international" analysis', *Journal of Education Policy*, Vol. 18, No. 1, pp. 1–17

Portner, H. (2008) *Mentoring New Teachers*, London: Sage

Priestley, M., Miller, K., Barrett, L. and Wallace, C. (2011) 'Teacher learning communities and educational change in Scotland: the Highland experience', *British Educational Research Journal*, Vol. 37, No. 2, pp. 265–84

Purdon, A. (2003) 'A national framework of CPD: continuing professional development or continuing policy dominance?', *Journal of Education Policy*, Vol. 18, No. 4, pp. 423–37

Purdon, A. (2004) 'Perceptions of the educational elite on the purpose of a national framework of continuing professional development (CPD) for teachers in Scotland', *Journal of Education for Teaching*, Vol. 30, No. 2, pp. 131–49

Putnam, R. D. and Feldstein, L. M. (2003) *Better Together*, New York: Simon and Schuster

Raffe, D. (2004) 'How distinctive is Scottish education? Five perspectives on distinctiveness', *Scottish Affairs*, No. 49, pp. 50–72

Raffe, D., Brannen, K., Croxford, L. and Martin, C. (1999) 'Comparing England, Scotland, Wales and Northern Ireland: the case for "home internationals" in comparative research', *Comparative Education*, Vol. 35, No. 1, pp. 9–25

Rees, G. (2007) 'The impacts of parliamentary devolution on education policy in Wales', *Welsh Journal of Education*, Vol. 14, No. 1, pp. 8–20

Reeves, J. (2008) 'Between a rock and a hard place? Curriculum for excellence and the quality initiative in Scottish schools', *Scottish Educational Review*, Vol. 40, No. 2, pp. 6–16

Reeves, J., Forde, C., O'Brien, J., Smith, P. and Tomlinson, H. (2002) *Performance Management in Education: Improving Practice*. London: Paul Chapman

Reeves, J., Turner, E., Morris, B. and Forde, C. (2003) 'Culture and concepts of school leadership and management: exploring the impact of CPD on aspiring headteachers', *School Leadership and Management*, Vol. 23, No. 1, pp. 5–24

Rhodes, C. and Brundrett, M. (2008) 'What makes my school a good training ground for leadership development? The perceptions of heads, middle leaders and classroom teachers from 70 contextually different primary and secondary schools', *Management in Education*, Vol. 22, No. 1, pp. 18–23

Riley, K. and Stoll, L. (2005) *Leading Communities: Purposes, Paradoxes and Possibilities*, London: Institute of Education

Rippon. J. H. and Martin, M. (2003) 'Supporting induction: relationships count', *Mentoring and Tutoring*, Vol. 11, No. 2, pp. 211–26

Rippon, J. H. and Martin, M. (2006) 'What makes a good induction supporter?', *Teaching and Teacher Education*, Vol. 22, No. 1, pp. 84–99

Robertson, J. (2008) *Coaching Educational Leadership*, London: Sage

Robertson, J. (2009) 'Coaching leadership learning through partnership', *School Leadership and Management*, Vol. 29, No. 1, pp. 39–49

Robinson, C. and Seba, J. (2004) *A Review of Research and Evaluation to Inform the Development of the New Postgraduate Professional Development Programme*, Brighton: Sussex Institute, University of Sussex

Sammons, P., Mujtaba, T., Earl, L. and Gu, Q. (2007) 'Participation in network learning community programmes and standards of pupil achievement: does it make a difference?', *School Leadership and Management*, Vol. 27, No. 3, pp. 213–38

Schön, D. (1983) *The Reflective Practitioner*, Aldershot: Ashgate

Schön, D. (1987) *Educating the Reflective Practitioner*, San Francisco: Jossey-Bass

Scottish Executive Education Department (SEED) (2000) *A Teaching Profession for the 21st Century* (McCrone Report), Edinburgh: Scottish Executive

Scottish Executive Education Department (2001) *A Teaching Professional for the 21st Century: Agreement Reached Following Recommendations Made in the McCrone Report*, Edinburgh: Scottish Executive

Scottish Executive Education Department (2002) *The Standard for Headship*, Edinburgh: Scottish Executive

Scottish Executive Education Department (2003) *Continuing Professional Development for Educational Leaders*, Edinburgh: Scottish Executive

Scottish Executive Education Department (2004) *Ambitious, Excellent Schools: Our Agenda for Action* (online). Available from: www.scotland.gov.uk/Publications/2004/11/20176/45852 (accessed 11 August 2010)

Scottish Executive Education Department (2005a) *Ambitious, Excellent Schools: The Standard for Headship*, Edinburgh: Scottish Executive

Scottish Executive Education Department (2005b) *Leadership: A Discussion Paper*, Edinburgh: Scottish Executive

Scottish Executive Education Department (2006) *Achieving the Standard for Headship – Providing Choice and Alternatives: A Consultation Document*, Edinburgh: Scottish Executive

Scottish Executive Education Department (2008) *Mentoring Teacher Education* (online). Available from: www.hmie.gov.uk/documents/publication/mite.html (accessed 10 December 2010)

Senge, P. M. (1990) *The Fifth Discipline: The Art and Practice of the Learning Organisation*, London: Century Business

Showers, B. and Joyce, B. (1996) 'The evolution of peer coaching', *Educational Leadership*, Vol. 53, No. 6, pp. 12–16

Simkins, T., Coldwell, M. Cailau, I., Finlyson, H. and Morgan, A. (2006) 'Coaching as an in-school leadership development strategy: experiences from leading from the middle', *School Leadership and Management*, Vol. 32, No. 3, pp. 321–40

Slater, L. (2008) 'Pathways to building leadership capacity', *Educational Management, Administration and Leadership*, Vol. 36, No. 1, pp. 55–69

Smith, A. (2007) 'Mentoring for experienced school principals: professional learning in a safe place', *Mentoring and Tutoring*, Vol. 15, No. 3, pp. 277–91

Smith, P. (2001) 'Mentors as gate-keepers: an exploration of professional formation', *Educational Review*, Vol. 53, No. 3, pp. 313–24

Snow-Gerono, J. L. (2004) 'Professional development in a culture of inquiry: PDS teachers identify the benefits of professional learning communities', *Teaching and Teacher Education*, Vol. 21, No. 3, pp. 241–56

SOEID (1998) *Proposals for Developing a Framework for Continuing Professional Development for the Teaching Profession in Scotland*, Consultation Document, Edinburgh: SOEID, 21 July

Spillane, J. (2006) *Distributed Leadership*, San Francisco: Jossey-Bass

Stenhouse, L. (1975) *An Introduction to Curriculum Research and Development*, London: Heinemann

Stenhouse, L. (1980) *Curriculum Research and Development*, London: Heinemann

Stoll, L., Bolam, R., McMahon, A., Wallace, M. and Thomas, S. (2006) 'Professional learning communities', *Journal for Educational Change*, Vol. 7, No. 4, pp. 221–58

Stoll, L. and Bolam, R. (2005) 'Developing leadership for learning communities', in Coles, M. J. and Southworth, G. (eds) (2005) *Developing Leadership: Creating the Schools of Tomorrow*, Maidenhead: Open University Press, pp. 50–64

Stoll, L. and Louis, K. S. (2007a) (eds) (2007a) *Professional Learning Communities: Divergence, Depth and Dilemmas*, Maidenhead: Open University Press

Stoll, L. and Louis, K. S. (2007b) 'Professional learning communities: elaborating new approaches', in Stoll and Louis (eds) (2007a), pp. 1–13

Stoll, L., Wallace, M., Bolam, R., McMahon, A., Thomas, S., Hawkey, K., Smith, M. and Greenwood, A. (2003) *Creating and Sustaining Effective Professional Learning Communities*, Annesley, Nottingham: DfES Publications

Strong, M. (2009) *Effective Teacher Induction and Mentoring*, New York: Teachers' College

Supovitz, J. (2002) 'Developing communities of instructional practice', *Teachers' College Record*, Vol. 104, No. 8, pp. 1591–1626

Sutherland, S. (1997) *Teacher Education and Training. Report 10 of the Dearing Report*, London: HMSO

Swaffield, S. (2004) 'Critical friends: supporting leadership, improving learning', *Improving Schools*, Vol. 7, No. 3, pp. 267–78

Taylor, W. (2008) 'The James Report revisited', *Oxford Review of Education*, Vol. 34, No. 3, pp. 291–311

Tickle, L. (2000) *Teacher Induction: The Way Ahead*, Buckingham: Open University Press

Tickle, L. (2001) 'Professional qualities and teacher induction', *Journal of In-Service Education*, Vol. 27, No. 1, pp. 51–64

Timperley, H. S. (2007) *Teacher Professional Learning and Development*, Brussels: The International Academy of Education

Timperely, H. S., Wilson, A., Barrar, H. and Fung, I. (2007) *Teacher Professional Learning and Development: Best Evidence Synthesis Iteration*, Wellington, New Zealand: Ministry of Education

Torrance, D. and Pritchard, I. (2010) *Developing Alternative Routes to School Headship: Evaluation of the University DARE 2 Programme, 2009–10*, Edinburgh: University of Edinburgh Centre for Educational Leadership

Torrance, H. and Pryor, J. (2001) 'Developing formative assessment in the classroom: using action research to explore and modify theory', *British Educational Research Journal*, Vol. 27, No. 5, pp. 667–83

Training and Development Agency for Schools (2006) *Professional Standards: Why Sit Still in Your Career?* London: TDA

Training and Development Agency for Schools (2009) *Strategy for the Professional Development of the Children's Workforce in Schools 2009–12*, London: TDA

Veenman, S., Denessen, E., Gerrits, J. and Kenter, J. (2001) 'Evaluation of a coaching programme for cooperating teachers', *Educational Studies*, Vol. 27, No. 3, pp. 317–40

Vescio, V., Ross, D. and Adams, A. (2008) 'A review of research on the impact of professional learning communities on teaching practice and student learning', *Teaching and Teacher Education*, Vol. 24, No. 1, pp. 80–91

Vygotsky, L. S. (1978) *Mind in Society: The Development of Higher Psychological Processes*, Cambridge, MA: Harvard University Press

Wales, S. (2003) 'Why coaching?', *Journal of Change Management*, Vol. 3, No. 3, pp. 275–82

West-Burnham, J. (2009) *Rethinking Educational Leadership: From Improvement to Transformation*, London: Continuum

Western SQH Flexible Route Handbook, Glasgow Western SQH Consortium

Whitmore, J. (2002) *Coaching For Performance: Growing People, Performance and Purpose*, third edn, London: Nicholas Brealey

Woods, P. A., Michael, C. and Woods, G. J. (2007) *Headteachers' Professional Development: Provision, Barriers and Need*, Aberdeen: University of Aberdeen for Learning and Teaching Scotland

Woolhouse, M. (2005) 'You can't do it on your own: gardening as an analogy for personal learning from a collaborative action research group', *Educational Action Research*, Vol. 13, No. 1, pp. 27–41

Zwart, R. C., Wubbels, T., Bergen, T. C. M. and Bolhuis, S. (2007) 'Experiences teacher learning within the context of reciprocal peer coaching', *Teachers and Teaching*, Vol. 13, No. 2, pp. 165–87

INDEX

Note: page numbers in *italics* denote figures or tables

Achinstein, B. 34, 42, 44
action research 8, 14, 25, 85, 87, 111
Ainscow, M. 77
Alcorn, M. 50
alternative approaches *58*
alternative approaches to mentoring 39–44
Ambitious, Excellent Schools: Our Agenda for Action (SEED) 50
American Confederation of Teachers 32
Appleby, R. 25
apprenticeship model 34, 36, 37
Argyris, C. 27, 47
Arnott, M. A. 2, 5
Asia-Pacific Economic Co-operation Ministerial Group 32
assessing roles 35
autonomous mode of learning 39, 83
autonomy, professional 12, 20

Baker Days 3
Ballet, K. 40, 42
Berglas, S. 84
Best Practice Research Scholarship 9
Black, D. R. 47
Blackman, A. 22, 49, 59, 60
Blair, T. 5
Bleach, K. 37
blended coaching model 49–50
blended learning approach 61
Bloom, G. 23, 50, 84
Bolam, R. 2, 13, 64, 65, 66, 68, 70, 75, 79
bonding process 66
Borgatti, S. P. 76, 78
boundary spanners 79, 80
bridging process 66
Brighouse, T. 9
Brookfield, S. D. 29, 41–2
Brown, S. 60
Brundrett, M. 46, 47, 48
Bryce, T. 2
Bubb, S. 33

Burley, S. 82–3
Bush, T. 46, 47, 62

Calderhead, J. 19
Callaghan, J. 5
capacity building 10, 46, 77, 79–80
career advancement 13, 19
Carroll, M. 16, 31, 42–3, 67, 71, 72
catchment area 65
change in practice
    boundary spanners 79, 80
    coaching-mentoring 21, 22, 23
    continuing professional development 7
    curricular developments 13
    evidence-informed 69, 75
    school community 66
    sharing knowledge 78
    willingness 60
Chapman, C. 63, 77
Chartered Teachers 11–12, 17, 28–9
Chi, M. T. H. 30
Christie, D. 12
Christie, F. 2, 12
Church, M. 76, 78
Clements, S. 3
Clough, P. 75
coach role 35, 57, 58–9
coaching
    classroom practice 21, 22, 23
    collaborative 23
    continuing professional development 49
    GROW model 49–50
    headship preparation programmes 49, 51
    leadership preparation 45, 46–7, 56–7
    limitations 82
    personal/intellectual development 84

reciprocity 85
Scottish Qualification for Headship
    48
student teachers 22
tutoring 55
coaching and mentoring approach 1–2,
    15–16, 17, 21–3, 61–2
coaching plus 57
Cochrane-Smith, M. 75
co-constructivist approach 30, 69, 78, 83
Coleman, M. 72
collaboration 70
    continuing professional development
        8
    personal development 10
    professional learning communities
        17, 42–3
    between schools 6, 10, 75–6
collaborative approaches
    coaching 23
    continuing professional development
        12, 14–15
    experienced practitioners/newer
        colleagues 18
    inter-teacher 8, 67, 80
    mentoring 42–3
    move towards 26–7
    student achievement 19
collaborative learning 27, 30–1, 63
collaborative professional enquiry 71–5
    cycles of 74
collective responsibility 68–9
co-mentoring 23
community, defined 65
competences, renewing/updating 13
conformity 34, 36, 83, 84, 86
Conlon,T. 6, 7–8
connection/partnerships 70
Construction Industry Council 4
continuing professional development
    (CPD) 1, 2, 4–5, 13
    barriers to participation 15
    career advancement 13
    change in practice 7
    coaching 49
    collaboration 8
    initial teacher education 29
    leadership 62
    mentoring 49
    Ofsted Report 71
    policy initiatives 6–12
    reviews 13–15, 71
    in USA 15

continuing teacher education 17–18
Costa, A. L. 24–5
Cowie, M. 12, 48, 61
Crawford, M. 47, 61
critical friends 23, 24–5
critical reflection 39, 47, 59, 83
criticality 28–9, 35, 41, 43–4, 82, 83
Cullingford, C. 34, 39
CUREE for DfES 9
A Curriculum for Excellence 12, 19

Dadds, M. 6, 7, 69, 74
Dahlgren, L. O. 25, 26
DARE 1 and 2 51, 52–3, 55–6, 58
Daresh, J. 19, 20
Darling-Hammond, L. 15
Daugherty, R. 1
Davidson, J. 49, 58
Davies, B. 47
Day, C. 4–5, 6, 8, 13
deficit model, newly qualified teachers 34,
    43
devolved school management 5
Devos, A. 35, 39
DfEE (Department for Educaton and
    Employment) 5, 9
DfES (Department for Education and
    Skills) 2, 9, 14, 75
dialogue 9, 71–2, 82, 83, 89, 90
discourse community 72
Donaldson, G. 88–9
Donaldson Report 88–9
Draper, J. 12, 34, 48
Driscoll, L. G. 24
DuFour, R. 17, 42
Durrant, J. 85
dynamics of model of learning 89

Earl, L. 47, 70, 75, 76, 77, 78, 79, 80
Earley, P. 22
Ecclestone, K. 84–5
Edinburgh University 51
education policy in devolution 1
education reform 5–6
Educational Institute for Scotland (EIS) 46
Ehrich, L. C. 20, 21
EIS (Educational Institute for Scotland) 46
Ellison, L. 47
emotional approaches, mentoring 20
emotional support 84
England
    educational reform 5
    Green Paper (1998) 8–9

Induction Standards 12
national framework for mentoring
and coaching 9–10
reviews of continuing professional
development 9, 13–15
enquiry-based learning 69
Eraut, M. 47
Evans, L. 3–4
executive coaching 21
experiential learning 28, 49
experiential methodologies 17–18, 19,
46–7, 82–90
experiential pedagogies 28, 84
experimentation 83–4
expertise 21, 30, 34, 42, 75

facilitation 29–31, 59
Farrell, T. 25
feedback as mirror 21–2
Feiman-Nemser, S. 13
Feldman, D. C. 59
Feldstein, L. M. 66
Finland 88
Finnie, G. 49, 50
5-14 Programme 13
Forde, C. 15, 18, 22, 34, 47, 48, 49–50, 54,
57, 89
Foster, P. C. 76, 78
Fournies, F. F. 49
Friedman, A. 4, 13
Fullan, M. 3, 77
Furlong, J. 5, 8–9

Ganser, T. 20–1, 83
Gates, P. 19
General Teaching Council for Scotland:
see GTCS
General Teaching Council for Wales: see
GTCW
Golby, M. 25
Green Paper (1998) 8–9
Gronn, P. 22, 31
Groundwater-Smith, R. 71
GROW model, coaching 49–50
GTCS (General Teaching Council for
Scotland)
on coaching and mentoring 50–1
leadership development 46
professional standards 28–9, 32
and Wales, compared 11
website 33
GTCW (General Teaching Council for
Wales) 5, 9, 11

Gu, Q. 6
Guile, D. 66, 70

Hadfield, M. 75
Hanbury, M. 22, 46, 48, 49, 55–6, 57, 62
Hargreaves, A. 67, 68, 77
Harland, J. 6, 7
Harris, A. 26
Hart, S. 69, 74
Hartley, J. 49
Hayes, D. 84–5
headship preparation programmes 11, 49,
51, 52–3
coaching and mentoring 52
headteachers
alternative preparation programme
48
as coaches 49, 59
as leaders 8, 46–7, 79–81
as managers 8
mentoring 50
professional learning communities
79
recruitment/retention crisis 46, 49
support 53
headteachers, aspiring
leadership development programmes
22, 62
mentoring 20
Standard for Headship 47, 51
support for 53, 62
Her Majesty's Inspectorate of Education
41, 45–6
Hewton, E. 3
Hextall, I. 5
Higher Still 13
Hinksman, B. 49
Hipp 42
Hobson, A. 23, 36, 38
Holden, G. 85
Holland 22
Hord, S. M. 42
Huffman, J. 42, 66, 80
Hulme, M. 12
Humes, W. 2
Hunt, G. 12
Hurling-Austin, L. 33–4, 83
Hustler, D. 13

improvement-focused interventions 75
inclusivity 69
induction 11, 12, 22, 32, 39–44
information and communication

technology 6, 13
Ingersoll, R. 83–4
initial teacher education 24, 29, 41, 43
innovation 1, 29, 83, 84
in-service training (INSET) 2–5
instruction, mentoring 59
Ives, Y. 21, 49

Jackson, D. 72, 76, 77, 78, 80
Jackson, P. 49
Jacobson, A. 80
James Report 2–3
Jones, M. 26
Joseph, K. 5
Joy, B. 22–3
Joyce, B. 26

Kallick, B. 24–5
Katz, S. 47, 70, 75, 76, 77, 78, 79, 80
Katzenmeyer, M. 80
Kelchtermans, G. 40, 42
Kennedy, A. 12, 14, 83
Kerwood, J. 3
Kinder, K. 6, 7
knowledge
    context-specific 78
    development of 28–9, 30
    sharing 78
    and skills 7
    socially distributed 70
knowledge-based paradigm 67
Kolb, D. A. 47, 82
Kralik, J. M. 83–4

Lankau, M. J. 59
Lave, J. 84
Le Cornu, R. 24
leadership 45–7, 62
    see also headteachers
Leadership: A Discussion Paper (SEED) 49
leadership development 16, 22, 45–7
leadership preparation
    coaching 45, 46–7, 56–7
    government-sponsored 47–8
    parity of esteem 60–1
    resourcing of 60–1, 62
    self-reflection 59–60
    see also headship preparation
        programmes
learner-driven meetings 20–1
learning 66
    closed system 84
    co-constructivist approach 69–70, 83
    culture of 10
    dynamics 89
    enquiry-based 69
    individual/collective 67
    professional 69–70, 71
    reciprocal 23
    situated 84
    transformative 83
learning communities 28
    see also professional learning
        communities (PLCs)
learning organisation 79
literacy and numeracy 9
Little, P. F. B. 26
Long, J. 39, 43
Lord, P. 87
Louis, K. S. 63, 76
Lu, H.-L. 26
Lumby, J. 72
Lytle, S. 75

MacBeath, J. 46
McIntyre, D. 60
McLean, M. 30
McMahon, A. 2, 41
Mahony, P. 5
managerialism 12
Martin, M. 15–16, 31, 36, 42, 64, 67, 79
Masters programmes in education 8, 11,
    47
medical educators 25, 26, 30
Menter, I. 48
mentor role 44, 57
mentoring 20–1
    alternative approaches 39–44
    collaborative approach 42–3
    continuing professional development
        49
    criticality 43–4
    headteachers 50
    induction 22, 32
    instruction 59
    limitations 82
    model of learning 34
    mutual 23
    newly qualified teachers 32–9
    problems with 35, 36
    Scottish Qualification for Headship
        48, 86
    sharing practice 83–4
    team approach 40–1
    USA 20
Mitchell, C. 64, 67, 68–9, 70

Moller, G. 80
Montgomery, A. 1
Moore, T. 24
Muijs, D. 70

National Assembly for Northern Ireland 1
National Assembly for Wales 1, 9
National College for Leadership of Schools and Children's Services (NCLSCS) 2
National College for School Leadership 75–9
National CPD Team 22
national framework for mentoring and coaching 9–10
National FRH 51, 52–4, 58
NCLSCS (National College for Leadersip of Schools and Children's Services) 2
Networked Learning Communities (NLCs) 75–9
Neville, A. J. 31
New Labour government 1, 5
New Opportunities Fund 6
New Professionalism 6
New Right 5
newly qualified teachers (newly qualified teachers) 2
    deficit model 34, 43
    mentoring 20, 32–6, 32–9
    probationary period 35
    professional development 33, 43, 44
    school politics 40, 42
    support mechanisms 32
Nutbrown, C. 75

O'Brien, J. 2, 12, 34, 48
observation of practice 20
OECD 48
Ofsted 9, 71
Opfer, D. 14–15
organisational learning 77
Oti, J. 24
Ozga, J. 2

partnerships 47–8, 70
Pask, R. 22–3
Paterson, L. 1
Patrick, F. 12
pedagogic excellence 12
Pedder, D. 15, 72
peer coaching 25–6
peer mentoring 24
peer-supported learning 17, 23–4, 46–7, 84
performativity 6, 9, 12

personal learning plan (PLP) 54, 55–6, 60
personal/intellectual development 10, 84
Phillips, M. 4, 13
Phillips, R. 2
placement request 65
PLCs: *see* professional learning communities
PLP (personal learning plan) 54, 55–6, 60
Pomphrey, C. 82–3
Portner, H. 34–5
Postgraduate Diploma 8
postgraduate school leadership development programmes 41
pre-service teacher education 26
Priestley, M. 12
primary teachers, male 24
Pritchard, I. 58, 62
probationer teachers 36, 42
problem-based learning (PBL) 30–1
process knowledge 47
Professional Development Bursaries 11
professional development of teachers
    government investment 2
    newly qualified 33, 43, 44
    process/product 4
    providers 6
    unplanned 8
    see also continuing professional development (CPD)
professional freedom 19
professional knowledge 59, 66–7
professional learning 18–20, 69–70
    coaching and mentoring 15
    components 82–3
    core process 86
    experiential methodologies 19
    individualised 85
    in-service training 2
    networked learning 76
    situated learning 84
professional learning communities (PLCs) 26–7
    characteristics of 68–79
    collaboration 17, 42–3
    and continuing professional development 16
    defined 63–7
    headteachers 79
    newly qualified teachers 43
    sharing expertise 17, 18
    sustained learning 40–1, 71–2
professional practice 18–19, 20, 29, 90
Pryor, J. 74

Purdon, A. 12
Putnam, R. D. 66

Qualified Teacher Status (QTS) 11

Raffe, D. 2
reciprocal learning 23
Rees, G. 1
Reeves, J. 12, 47, 48, 62, 71, 89
reflection 26, 27, 29, 82, 86, 90
reflective practitioner 19, 87
relating roles 35
Rhodes, C. 46
Riley, K. 63, 65, 77, 79
Rippon, J. H. 36, 42
Robertson, J. 48, 59, 60, 61, 85–6
Robinson, C. 71

Sackney, L. 64, 67, 68–9, 70
Sammons, P. 69, 70
scaffolding 30, 72
Scandinavian countries 88
Schön, D. 27, 29, 47
School Boards 5
school community 65–6
school governance 46
school improvement project 52–3
school managers 51
school politics 39, 40, 42
Scotland
    Chartered Teachers 11–12, 17
    collaboration between schools 6
    continuing professional development
        standards 12
    distinctiveness of education 2
    School Headship 12
    teacher education 88
    Teacher Induction 12, 15–16, 32–3
    Teacher Research Scholarships 11
    see also GTCS (General Teaching
        Council for Scotland)
Scottish Executive 19, 50–1
Scottish Executive Education Department
    (SEED)
    Ambitious, Excellent Schools: Our
        Agenda for Action 50
    continuing professional development
        12–13
    framework for educational
        leadership 46, 47
    HMIe 41
    Leadership: A Discussion Paper 49
    teacher induction 32, 41

Teaching Profession for the 21st
    Century 45–6
    see also GTCS (General Teaching
        Council for Scotland)
Scottish Office Education and Industry
    Department (SOEID) 13
Scottish Parliament 1
Scottish Qualification for Headship (SQH)
    17, 20, 46, 47–8, 51
Seba, J. 71
self-reflection 59–60
Senge, P. M. 63, 77, 79
shadowing of mentor 20
shared values 68
sharing practice 78, 83–4, 86
Showers, B. 26
Simkins, T. 22
situated learning 84
Slater, L. 48
Smith, A. 1, 24
Smith, P. 37–8
Snow-Gerono, J. L. 27
social engineering 84–5
social network theory 76–7
socialisation 33, 34
SOEID (Scottish Office Education and
    Industry Department) 13
Spillane, J. 80
SQH (Scottish Qualification for Headship)
    20, 46, 48, 86
Standard for Active Registration 88
Standard for Chartered Teacher 28–9
Standard for Full Registration 28–9, 32
Standard for Headship 28–9, 46, 47, 50,
    51, 52
Standard for Initial Teacher Education
    28–9
Stenhouse, L. 24
Stoll, L. 26, 63, 64, 65, 66, 68, 69, 70, 76,
    77, 79
Street, H. 72
Strong, M. 34
student standards, raising 8, 71
Supovitz, J. 27
Sutherland, S. 8
Swaffield, S. 25

Taylor, F. 50
Taylor, W. 2
teacher education 5–6, 22, 88
    see also initial teacher education
teacher identity 40, 42
teacher induction

mentoring 49, 86
Scotland 12, 15–16, 32–3
teachers as mentors 87
USA 83
teacher injury 12
teacher learning 40–1, 82–90
teacher learning communities 86
Teacher Research Scholarships 11
Teachers Development Agency 10
Teaching Profession for the 21st Century
(SEED) 45–6
Teaching Scotland's Future (Donaldson) 88
Temperley, J. 76, 77, 78, 80
theories/knowledge 19
therapeutic education 84–5
threads/knots/nets framework 76–7, 78
Tickle, L. 12, 34
Timperley, H. S. 19, 86
Torrance, D. 16, 31, 48, 58, 62, 74
Training and Development Agency for
Schools 87
trust, mutual 68
tutor role 57
tutoring 29–31, 30, 48, 55

United States of America 15, 20, 83
universities 51, 87

value congruence 7, 68
Veenman, S. 22
Vescio, V. 27
visits/exchanges 11
Vygotsky, L. S. 72

Wales 9, 11
see also National Assembly for Wales
Wales, S. 21
Weindling, D. 13
Wenger, E. 84
West, M. 77
West-Burnham, J. 66, 68, 76
Western SQH Consortium Flexible Route
51, 52–3, 54–5, 58
Whitmore, J. 49
Woods, P. A. 46, 61
Woolhouse, M. 72

Young, M. 66, 70

zone of proximal development 72
Zwart, R. C. 25–6